# STRESS BURNOUT DECODED

UNDERSTANDING THE CYCLE OF STRESS TO BUILD
RESILIENCE AND THRIVE FOR A MORE FULFILLING
LIFE IN 14 DAYS OR LESS

HARMONY BROOKS

# CONTENTS

# INTRODUCTION

It's 5:45 a.m.; your alarm goes off, making your heart sink with the anguish of yet another tough day on Earth. You shout out, "FIVE MORE MINUTES, PLEASE," before you hit the snooze button and lay in bed, contemplating whether to get up. However, ditching your daily duties soon becomes unthinkable, so you give yourself a pep talk before getting up and preparing for the day.

Your muscles are stiff, your head is aching, and your brain is fogged. But the thought of losing your job or missing that critical class haunts you, so you persevere through all the fatigue and discomfort.

Minutes before your cab arrives, you grab your coffee —the only thing that has kept you going—and quickly exit the house. As you step out of the house and into the cab, you come to realize that your rough mornings are only a fraction of what's still to come.

Young adulthood is often fraught with endless challenges. What's worse is the age-old stereotypes that place young people at the top of the list of people who are less susceptible to stress. It can be challenging to stay afloat when your whole life feels like it's falling apart right before your eyes.

Waking up in the morning feeling unmotivated to go through another hectic day and going to bed late feeling unaccomplished despite already having done so much can really take a toll on your mental health. Stress burnout is a damaging experience for ourselves and those around us. It can be frustrating, I know, because I, too, have found myself in that exact situation.

A little less than five years ago, I found myself in a terrible space in my life. I was just a few months shy of 21 and starting out my new life as an adult in the bustling city of New York. On the exterior, anyone would have sworn that my life was taken straight out of a fairy tale.

I was a full-time employee at a call center, a successful student who was equally a social butterfly. However, underneath all that glistening glory was a girl trembling under the pressure of a highly demanding life. And trying to keep up with this only eventually led to a breaking point.

As fate would one day have it, the cracks in my carefully constructed facade began to unveil themselves. Juggling the demands of my social life, school, and work made me spiral downward. I felt like I was drowning in a sea of obligations created by my over-ambitiousness and other things I couldn't control. I knew that I immediately had to do something before I lost my sense of self.

Having experienced stress burnout firsthand, I know how hopeless and desperate life can get. However, I want to remind you it's always possible to turn that around and claim captaincy over your life. You can still go out there and conquer the world with a stress-free mind!

My battles with stress burnout have motivated me to share my story and help those in the same situation, so I decided to write this book. After nights of endless research, I finally came across a few excellent resources for the cause, and all of these, I have put with love and care in one place for your use.

Within the pages of this book awaits the answer to your stress and mental unrest. I will walk you through some practical steps you can take to initiate your journey to a better and more fulfilling life. You will learn how to build emotional resilience amid the storm and face life's many challenges head-on without jeopardizing your mental health.

In addition to that, you will also discover a haven of mindfulness and meditation practices that you can incorporate into your life and find reprieve from the mental turmoil imposed by life.

But it doesn't end there. This serves as not only a resource to help you enhance your mental health but also to improve your physical health. Since physical exercise is the gateway to mental well-being, you will learn how to make it your greatest weapon in the fight against stress. The best part is that you don't have to lose hope waiting for a result; your new life is within reach.

You can rediscover yourself and carve out a life of balance using the techniques in only 14 days or less! So, the wait is over, and the time is now to relinquish all the stress that you have been harboring. The time is now to reclaim your life and enjoy it once again. I encourage you to take a stand against stress burnout and to embark on this 14-day road to recovery. You are more than capable of changing this painful narrative written through the lens of stress into a fruitful and joyful life story. All you need to do is believe that you are worthy of happiness and freedom from mental slavery. Without further ado, let us move right into the first chapter, where we will discuss all about the stress epidemic.

1

# THE STRESS EPIDEMIC

Did you know that in 2020, 7 out of 10 American adults claimed that they had been under significant levels of stress? To top that, they claimed this led them to become unproductive tired, and harbor an overwhelming sense of dissatisfaction over their lives (American Psychological Association, 2020).

The stress levels among Americans have been shooting out the roofs, leaving many people feeling desperate and uncertain about their futures.

Often, many people are left puzzled and unable to really point out a single cause of their stress. This is mainly because no single reason is to blame. There are many inconclusive reasons as to why you can suffer from stress, and to start healing from this issue, the best way to start is by being aware of all the things that could trigger stress.

This is precisely what we will be discussing in this chapter. By the end of this chapter, you will have a clearer picture of what stress is and the different ways it can manifest in your life. So,

without waiting any longer, let us discuss the biology of stress.

## THE BIOLOGY OF STRESS

"I'm so stressed" and "I can't afford to be stressed" are all common phrases used every day involving the word "stress." Undeniably, it is an excruciatingly painful part of life, but what does it really mean? Stress is the result of any internal or external factor formally known as a stressor that brings forth a string of adverse responses from our bodies. While life isn't perfect all the time, and we are bound to get stressed occasionally, the actual harm is prolonged stress. Being stressed continually can alter the normal functioning of our bodies and how we get by in day-to-day life.

The effects of stress go far beyond making you forget where you placed your car key or feel like your world is upside-down. Stress can pose severe dangers to your health that you probably won't realize until it's too late; some of these are physiologically damaging.

The following case study explains how stress can affect your psychological well-being.

It's totally normal to be tired after a long day of hard work or when you didn't get enough sleep. However, when you are constantly tired without much reason, it's a cause for concern. One of the most prevalent outcomes of prolonged stress is chronic fatigue.

In a particular study, it was uncovered that 25% of the subjects were constantly exhausted as a result of stress (Blain, 2022). Further investigation revealed that fatigue caused by stress stems from issues such as a hectic schedule and too little time to rest.

It is essential to know that stress usually doesn't happen on its own; there is a more complex logic behind it. Just like a car would need an engine to propel it, stress also has a driving factor behind it. Let's look at this in more detail.

### *What Are Stress Hormones and Why Should You Care?*

Stress hormones are chemicals that help us fight or avoid danger in life-threatening situations, commonly referred to as a fight or flight mechanism (Harvard Health Publishing, 2020). During highly stressful times, these hormones (cortisol, adrenaline, epinephrine, and norepinephrine) are released to increase blood sugar, breathing, and heart rates. As the breathing rate and blood sugar increase, the heart can pump more oxygen and energy to the muscle cells, equipping them to fight the danger or escape the threat.

While this mechanism would have been helpful in the Stone Age, when our chances of being approached by a lion or a crocodile were higher, it doesn't serve its intended purpose in modern life.

Modern-day civilization has protected us from most life-threatening dangers, so there is barely a need for our bodies to activate this fight-or-flight response.

Nonetheless, civilization has also introduced numerous stressors that can still trigger this response. So, while they may not necessarily pose a threat to our lives, our brains perceive them as such, leading to the inevitable release of these hormones triggering the response in situations where it isn't needed.

Let's take, for instance, being stuck in a traffic jam and running late for work. While finding yourself in this position can be downright frustrating, it doesn't warrant the activation of this mechanism.

With all that said, the real danger lies in the fact that modern-day life is inherently stressful, and the continuous release of stress hormones can send the body into overdrive.

When the secretion of these hormones becomes regular, they accumulate in our systems and cause significant harm.

Instead of your heart beating fast only to provide your cells with energy in emergencies, it beats fast even when there isn't an immediate threat. This can lead to a litany of health conditions, such as anxiety, depression, and high blood pressure, to name a few.

Now that you understand how stress hormones work and affect our bodies adversely let us look at the steps of stress and how stress manifests in our bodies in more detail.

While it is widely acknowledged that individuals who suffer from stress exhibit strong emotional reactions, a 2013 study conducted by neuroscientists reveals just how little stress is needed to set someone's emotional reactions ablaze (Harvard Health Publishing, 2020).

In the study, a small group of individuals were educated on the various coping mechanisms that they could employ to deal with stress. Shortly after, they had their hands dipped into freezing water and were exposed to a series of explicit images of cold-blooded animals such as snakes and lizards.

Besides being recently equipped with stress coping mechanisms, they still couldn't control their emotional responses due to the stress they acquired from dipping their hands in icy water.

This study really showed that stress is more concerning than we perceive it to be and that even the slightest of stressors, such as those we face in daily life, can significantly affect our ability to control our emotions (Harvard Health Publishing, 2020).

So, now the question stands: if slight stressors have such a notable impact on our psychological well-being, then how big of an impact do major stressors have on us?

### How Does Stress Affect Our Psychological Health?

Stress manifests in several ways in our lives, both good and bad. You may or may not know that when stress is slight and sporadic, it can make you feel energetic, motivated, and strengthen your critical thinking skills.

Let's say, for instance, you have been looking for employment for months, and you finally get a call informing you to come in for an interview tomorrow. This is exciting, right? This anticipation can motivate you to take action quickly, do research on your goals and objectives of the company, tweak your resume to reflect the requirements of the company, and rehearse your responses.

This stress has good psychological impacts that lead to good outcomes in your life.

On the other hand, chronic stress can lead to opposite consequences. When stress is a way of life, it can have extremely harmful effects on your mental health, affecting how you think, feel, approach problems, and live your life in general. This is why it is important to address stress before it gets its way with you. Here are some ways stress can impair your mental health and behavior:

- **Lack of motivation:** A stressed mind cannot bring itself to focus on anything. Being stressed for a lengthy period can lead to a negative perception of life. Usually, this can be seen as a lack of motivation or inspiration to do anything.
- **Memory issues:** Forgetfulness is a common symptom of stress. Stress hormones often interfere with the hippocampus, a region in the brain responsible for managing memory.
- **Sleep patterns:** The constant activation of the body's stress response system can make it almost impossible for the body and mind to

relax and unwind. This makes it challenging to fall asleep and stay asleep, affecting your overall quality of sleep. Consequently, you may suffer from sleep disorders such as insomnia and fragmented sleep.

- **Trouble controlling emotions:** A result of a stressful lifestyle is difficulty in regulating emotions. This is because the part of the brain responsible for managing emotional responses gradually diminishes as a result of stress.
- **Fatigue:** Having to deal with an influx of stressors and worries daily can be extremely draining for the mind. This state of mental exhaustion then translates outward as physical fatigue.
- **Social withdrawal:** Stress can cause you to lose interest in being in the company of others and a general dislike for social selection. You may find yourself avoiding people or public areas.

The psychological impacts of stress can make it challenging to cope sufficiently with life. At times, this can drive people to resort to substance abuse as a means of venting out their frustration, which also aids further in mental deterioration. Oftentimes, unresolved mental unrest can lead to the manifestation of more severe problems, such as mental health issues.

### *Stress-Related Mental Illnesses*

While stress itself isn't an ailment, it is a leading cause of a wide range of mental disorders, like anxiety, depression, and PTSD. However, that isn't all. It can also aggravate existing symptoms of mental illness, making the condition tenfold worse.

The following is Alliana's narrative on how she acquired mental illness as a result of stress.

Twenty-six-year-old Aliana's life is nothing short of hectic. She works a highly demanding nine-to-five and has a calendar full of other personal commitments. Initially, she was able to cope; however, as time passed, she found herself bogged down by her never-ending responsibility, and this took a severe toll on her mental well-being, putting her on the road to stress and, ultimately, a mental illness diagnosis.

It started with an overwhelming sense of worry that she couldn't shake off. The combination of work deadlines and problems in her personal life evoked restlessness in her.

Her sleep was riddled with persistent thoughts of unfinished work, and regardless of what she tried, she couldn't fall asleep. Her once joyful aura diminished as she increasingly became immersed in a pool of sadness and mental turmoil.

Aliana used to pride herself in her determination to succeed and impressive track record at work. But suddenly, her quality work vanished down the tubes as she often felt unmotivated to work.

Aliana perceived her situation to be something in passing, and although she knew she was stressed, she believed she would soon get better. However, the issue was that the sources of her stress were left unsolved.

Her stress continued to prevail and take over her life. Aliana's body started to shut down slowly; she had constant headaches and chronic fatigue, and she found herself breaking into tears all too frequently. One day, she came home under a serious panic attack, which had her trembling, sweating, and gasping for air.

This was instantly picked up by her parents, who were shocked at the terrible state their daughter was in. Luckily, they were able to decode the signs of help that her body was desperately trying to convey as stress.

After sitting her down and talking through the matter with her, they finally convinced her to go and see a doctor.

The very next day, Aliana set an appointment with a therapist who specializes in stress-related disorders. After going through extensive analyses and assessments, it was finally laid before her—she had been diagnosed with an anxiety disorder and depression. A shell-shocked Aliana, who only went to the therapist to get help for her stress, left with two serious mental health illnesses, both stemming from her chronic stress.

As much as it came as a surprise to her, it was also a significant turning point in her life. It was as if a weight had been lifted off her shoulders, and she didn't feel stuck anymore. Aliana focused her efforts on finding solutions to her conditions and getting better. Eventually, after many afternoons of venting at the therapist's office, she finally had a grip on her life and was looking in a more positive direction.

As seen in Aliana's story, numerous stressors often work together, causing stress. While the list is inconclusive, one of the two most prevalent reasons for stress among young adults is societal and workplace factors.

### *What Societal and Workplace Factors Lead To Stress and How Does This Happen*

Due to the high cost of living in modern life, for most of us, a job is of utmost importance. Although employment cushions us financially, it equally brings its fair share of stress into our lives. This is something that has been recognized worldwide. In fact, work has been listed by many people among the top stressors (Personnel Today, 2016).

So, while work-related stress may not necessarily be your sole stressor, chances are high that it counts as one of them. In order for you to deal with your stress accordingly, it is vital that you get a complete understanding of all the factors that could contribute to your work-derived stress. Furthermore, a clear understanding of where this stress stems from is also helpful in forming a powerful defense against it.

This brings us to ask, *what is work stress, and how exactly does it affect us?*

To be honest, work-related stress does not look the same for everyone; however, there is some common basis on which it can be defined. One way to define it is as an imbalance between work pressures and one's ability to deal with them.

When this happens, you may find yourself bogged down by a lot of tasks you are unable to fulfill, and this can be extremely stressful.

The most toxic working conditions that frequently push people into a corner are stringent deadlines and high turnaround corporations. These situations have taken away the human element of work and instead placed unrealistic expectations for employees to live up to.

This constant overdrive with very little time to recuperate eventually leads to burnout, which has taxing health consequences.

In fact, one such work realm that has been responsible for placing extreme amounts of pressure on employees is the healthcare sector. It has been reported that a significant number of nurses have resigned as a result of workplace stress and burnout (Personnel Today, 2016).

Although workplace stress on its own is a type of stress, there are a few other factors that mount to what we eventually refer to as "workplace stress." Nonetheless, it is also important to note that what stresses you may not necessarily stress another person. But, with that said, there is a list of everyday workplace stressors that most people have cited for their mental unrest:

- **Nature of tasks:** Tedious, time-consuming, and perplexing tasks can make it difficult to execute our jobs effectively and reduce productivity. Often, this leads to one feeling like they are not doing their job correctly and decreases their confidence on the job.
- **Management style:** A good management team allows employees to work freely without much stress. Conversely, not ideal management can

pile up work for you to do in a limited amount of time, making you feel doomed.

- **Work relationships:** Toxic co-worker relationships can cause stress on an individual. When workers constantly rub each other the wrong way and quarrel, it can reduce one's confidence and make their job a lot more complicated than it already is.
- **A lack of boundaries:** Not effectively setting your boundaries can cause you to take on more tasks than you can handle. As a result of this, you may find yourself spreading thin, trying to juggle too many tasks at once. Failure to accomplish these tasks can lead to stress.
- **Future concerns:** Any magnitude of uncertainty over your career's future can be a cause of stress. Whether it is working in a single position without getting a promotion or if you lack job security as a result of working in a volatile environment, all these factors are significant stressors.

With that said, it is important to know the signs of workplace stress to be able to identify them. Here are some of the most prevalent signs:

- Struggling to concentrate on tasks.

- Reduced self-confidence and feelings of worthlessness.
- Persistent headaches and migraines.
- Chronic exhaustion.

Workplace stress can have multidimensional effects that can cause serious harm to our quality of life. This is because the stress caused by your work obligations can also infiltrate into other parts of your life, affecting them negatively. A good example of this is the disruption of the work-life balance.

Stressors in the workplace can hamper your productivity and progress; as a result, you may find yourself taking home several unfinished tasks. Instead of spending time with your friends and family, you become engulfed in getting work done. And this can be extremely damaging to your personal relationships. Furthermore, you also give up self-care and doing things that once made you happy, which can stress you out even further. Similarly, societal factors can also be a source of stressors. Let us look further into that.

## How Do Societal Factors Lead to Stress

A major driving factor of humanity is social connectedness. Social interaction stimulates the release of "happy" hormones such as oxytocin, which can counteract stress hormones. This is why it is vital to maintain good relations with those closest to us; however, sometimes life doesn't always give us this on a silver platter. As much as we are social beings, life gets in the way, making it difficult to keep ourselves connected to others.

There are many reasons why that can be, but the main reasons are attributed to social pains such as loneliness, marital issues, and family conflict.

It can be difficult to vent out concerns and problems when we don't have the best relationships with the people closest to us. A lack of a solid support system can lead to the bottling up of emotions and ruminating over problems, which all result in stress (Bakhuys Roozeboom et al., 2020).

Another important issue that must be brought to light is the role mental illnesses, such as anxiety and depression, have in our social standing. While it has already been mentioned that stress is a gateway to mental illness, mental illness is also a source of stress.

Such conditions lead to people shutting the world out as they withdraw from everyone. As their social system grows smaller, and they have no one to talk to, they become lonelier and more exposed to stress.

However, the list of societal issues that can lead to stress is limitless and ongoing. The following are some other causes of societal stress:

- **Financial stress:** Financial instability and debt can lead to stress.
- **Social expectations:** Constant pressures to be on par with certain behaviors and standards are harmful to one's peace of mind.
- **Discrimination and inequality:** Discrimination based on sexual orientation, race, and gender is damaging to one's self-esteem.

All these factors eventually lead people to withdraw from the world or become isolated, thus leading to social stress.

This brings us to the end of this chapter. I hope that you now have a broadened understanding of what stress is and how it can impact your life. Stress is a multifaceted issue that calls for early action. To do so, you need to be cognizant of all the ways it can impact your life. Stressors range from workplace-related all the way to societal issues, and knowing exactly what it is that is spurring your mental decline is crucial in finding a solution and acting proactively.

Now, you can use this newfound knowledge of stress as your greatest ally in your journey to recovery. This knowledge serves as a stepping stone to a new life of health and happiness and as an important weapon in challenging the cycle of stress. This is what we will be discussing in the next chapter.

2

---

# THE CYCLE OF STRESS

Stress is an unfortunate part of life that quite honestly makes us dread living. If it's not dealt with quickly and effectively, it can become an ongoing cycle that inflicts multiple issues. Besides knowing what the various causes of stress are, it is essential to understand what stresses you.

This will point you in the right direction as to what you can do to neutralize the effects of these stressors.

This is precisely the main point of this topic. We will be focusing on how you can evaluate your situation and identify your personal stressors. By the end of this chapter, you will have a vivid picture of how your stress manifests and be better equipped to take actionable steps against it. Let's delve right into it.

## IDENTIFYING PERSONAL STRESSORS

One way to effectively describe stress is as a hurricane or a whirlwind, causing damage to anything it passes and leaving our lives in turmoil. This is something that can have lingering effects for many people, with one thing leading to another and eventually a total mental breakdown. The following is Mandy's almost life-long story of stress.

Looking back at the life I once led, I'm still dumbfounded by the fact that people thought my life was a dream. Although I was young, beautiful, and held a lot of other admirable qualities, inside lay a battery of unresolved issues.

Ever since my teenage years, my life was defined by a sequence of debilitating setbacks, which, in combination, all played a massive part in leaving my mental health in shambles.

My childhood was nothing short of a series of sexual abuse cases and mental and physical abuse. All these events contributed to my stress levels and sucked out all the joy I had in my life.

I spent a greater part of my life worried about what could happen next. At times, it got so intense that I became afraid to leave my home.

My stress levels and anxiety forced me to eventually call it quits on my modeling career, staying home and crying my eyes out each day. I knew that something was wrong but denied that I needed help. In some instances, I would dismiss all past fears as mere exaggerations.

After having suffered from stress for almost all my life, I finally decided to get help at the age of 35 years old. The doctor told me that had I reached out earlier, my stress probably wouldn't have gotten this bad. Through a series of sessions, he taught me how to identify my stressors as well as how I could deal with them appropriately.

Getting help has helped me to deal with my stress a lot better than I previously did. Each time I feel stressed, I am quickly able to spot the reason behind my stress and use applicable methods to alleviate it.

I have since led a much more fulfilling and joyful life, and it was all because I decided to take action.

As seen in Mandy's story, unresolved stress can span on and on for decades, taking a toll on your mental health and disrupting your normal way of life. This is why taking a step back to analyze the situation in the midst of stress is crucial to reflect and uncover the root cause or causes of your predicament.

### *Self-Reflecting and Identifying Stressors*

Nothing is too small a stressor. Stress can stem from literally anything. While we are better able to pinpoint stressors such as a heavy workload, financial instability, and relationship conflict, there are subtle stressors that often go unnoticed.

Others are external, while others are internal. An external subtle stressor would be, for example, receiving a wrong order or waiting to be attended to for a long time at the bank. Internal stressors would be feeling the need to act a certain way and beating yourself up when you don't or being extremely competitive to the point that it kills your morale.

For these reasons, it is always best to self-reflect and find the potential causes of your stress. Questions like: Why do I feel anxious today? My mind is not settled; what could be the cause? And why do I feel so down?

When self-reflecting, it is always important, to be honest with yourself and avoid dismissing potential stressors as "not big enough to cause stress."

With that said, it is also important to identify what can and cannot be controlled. If, for instance, you work from home and constant notifications and noise around the house are keeping you from getting any work done. You can try to block notifications while you work and find a designated area where you can work without any interruptions.

Furthermore, categorizing your stressors according to controllable and uncontrollable will help you slowly eliminate stress from your life and devise management strategies for issues that are out of your hands. The following are stressors that can be controlled:

- workload
- time management
- organization and planning
- exercise, nutrition, and body image
- social interactions and relationships
- sleep habits
- financial management
- screen time and social media use
- your immediate surroundings

Stressors that you cannot control include:

- other people's behaviors
- traffic
- political and societal issues
- economic failure and job loss
- death and loss of a loved one
- unforeseeable accidents and injuries
- the past

Identifying your stressors can be hard to do at times; however, there are many ways of getting down to the problem. One recommended technique for doing so is journaling. Take time from your day to journal. Although this can be any time of the day, it is best to do it at the day's end, just before bed. Journaling doesn't have to be anything hectic. In fact, it can be as simple as making a note on your smartphone. When journaling, it is important to reflect on stressful moments and their possible triggers.

There are also physical and mental indicators of stress, such as achy muscles, headaches, sadness, or anxiety that you may be feeling.

You can also evaluate whether your stress is stemming from a major life change or something else.

Identifying your stressors is a big step in your road to recovery and a game changer that will impact your life going forward. Furthermore, you will be better knowledgeable as to what steps you can take.

### *Mitigating Common Stressors*

Preventing the occurrence of stress is not an easy task; in fact, in most cases, it is impossible. However, how you mitigate your stress can go a long way. Stress doesn't affect everyone the same, as we all have different stress thresholds, but the ways we can minimize it stay constant. Consider the following as ways to do this:

- **Self-Care:** Find something you can do to de-stress. This could be listening to music, watching your favorite movie, or making your favorite meal. Alternatively, you can engage in your old hobbies or create new ones. This will serve as a distraction and take your mind off the stress.

- **Eat well and exercise frequently:** Stress can cause a reduced appetite in some people and, in others, an increase, especially cravings for sugary and fatty foods. This can only lead to more stress. It becomes a vicious cycle. Instead, opt for wholesome foods such as fruits, vegetables, and fish, which are high in omega-3. Exercising regularly can also help to release stress and improve overall mental and physical health.

- **Positive Mindset:** Practice gratitude for all the good things your life has to offer and avoid ruminating on negativity.

- **Letting Go:** Sometimes, we get caught up in wanting everything to be perfect. Learn to let go and accept things you can't control.

- **Limit Caffeine and Alcohol:** These substances may offer a temporary 'fix', but they also have the potential to aggravate stress. They make things worse in the long run.
- **Nature:** Go out and let the sunshine on you and breathe in the fresh air. The vitamins that come with the sunshine have been proven to help counter stress and boost moods.
- **Solicit social support:** Never be ashamed to reach out to family and friends for assistance. It's always good to have someone to talk to and ask for advice. Social interaction can improve moods drastically.

Working in the healthcare sector has been reported to be one of the most emotionally and physically taxing careers. A group of healthcare professionals was interviewed on how they dealt with the pressure and stress that came with their jobs and how effective they felt these coping strategies were (Reilly et al., 2021). Below are some findings of the interview.

- 88.63% coped with their stress by engaging in some sort of enjoyable pastime activity or hobby.
- 77.82% spent time with family and friends as a way of getting rid of stress.

- 72.64% exercised regularly.

The overall verdict was that these coping mechanisms were typically helpful in reducing stress.

Bottling up stress only leads to more stress—you can look at it as a snowball effect.

You can use all the above methods to help you relax and gain back control over your life.

### What Are Unhealthy Coping Mechanisms

Stress can, at times, put us in a state of desperation and in search of immediate solutions. Unfortunately, some of these 'solutions' to stress aren't so healthy or sustainable. These are referred to as unhealthy coping mechanisms, and while they can provide temporary relief from emotional unrest, they have harmful long-term effects.

Unhealthy stress coping mechanisms do not correct the underlying cause of the problem but cause a person to avoid dealing with it. For this reason, they are not at all helpful when it comes to mitigating stress; instead, they can string along many complications with them, which may lead to even more stress.

To avoid the continuation of an endless cycle of stress and unhappiness, it is important to gain awareness of the negative ways of dealing with stress.

**Self-Harm**

Even though some people find relief in the pain that comes with cutting or burning themselves, this is not a sustainable way of handling stress. Rather, it only inflicts harm on your physical and emotional health.

**Substance Abuse**

It's never advisable to seek emotional solace in drugs and alcohol. Being intoxicated can serve as a distraction from stress, but it is essential to remember that this can only lead to addiction and harmful behaviors and damage your relationship with those closest to you, among other consequences.

**Binge or Emotional Eating**

It may be comforting to eat a bag of chips and sip on a can of Coke when you are distraught; however, this can lead to the accumulation of fat around your organs (visceral fat), which can impair their function and lead to obesity. Don't get me wrong, you can enjoy your Coke, but anything in excess is harmful to the body.

## Emotional Undereating

Just like binge eating is harmful, eating too little in response to stress can also have serious consequences. No matter how stressful life gets, be sure to maintain healthy eating habits.

## Isolating Yourself

It's very common to want to be left alone when you are sad or stressed; most of us crave to be alone during times like this. However, a lack of social interaction can minimize social support and worsen stress.

## Acting Impulsively

Splurging money, calling up your ex, and reckless driving can get your mind off stress for a little while but can have harsh consequences to follow. As tempting as it may be to seek momentary relief and act on a whim when you are stressed, it is always important to look at the situation wholly and objectively. This way, you can keep yourself from falling into a downward spiral or initiating your demise.

The above listed gives you a good overview of what to avoid when dealing with stress. Unfortunately, some people fall victim to these unhealthy behaviors and live to regret them. Twenty-three-year-old Collin is one of those people; let us take a moment to read through his story.

After losing his best friend, Charles, to a tragic car accident, Collin's life was plagued by immense pressure.

He couldn't bring himself to accept his new reality, so he turned to the reprieve of substance abuse and clubbing.

Collin joined the wrong group of friends and went partying every night, sometimes even using the last of his money. The drugs and alcohol he indulged in at the club often led him to do a couple of regrettable things, some of which were irreversible. When he got intoxicated, he would do things he would later regret and sometimes not even remember.

This got so bad that he started to lose friendships because he wasn't the same fun person he once was. None of these "attempts" to relinquish his stress served him any justice because once he sobered up and returned to reality, his stress still haunted him. On top of that was his unrelenting addiction to drugs and alcohol, which caused conflict between him and his family.

After a full week of partying and partaking in unhealthy behaviors, Collin woke up feeling extremely ill. He thought he'd just caught a minor cold and that he would be fine within a day or two. But a week went by, and his condition was only getting worse. It was getting unbearable, and he decided to go for a check-up. At the doctor's office, he had a few blood tests done to determine the source of his illness.

To his horror, his doctor told him that he was developing a deadly lung disorder that needed him to change his lifestyle and take care of his health.

Collin couldn't believe how far his avoidance of dealing with the direct cause of his stress had led him.

He was determined to change his life and get back into a healthy state.

Collin gave up the clubbing, the drugs, and alcohol and focused on addressing the exact cause of his stress— losing his best friend.

He decided to exercise regularly and use physical fitness as an outlet for his emotional distress. Furthermore, he decided to journal his emotions as a way of addressing his pain.

As the days went by, Collin could feel a great sense of relief. It was like walking out into a field of flowers on a sunny day after being cooped up in a dark cave for years, and this wasn't something he was willing to give up.

## *Dealing With Workplace Stress: Breaking the Cycle One Step at a Time*

If you are a full-time employee, then you are probably well-acquainted with the frustration of having to deal with a nagging boss. A colleague who doesn't want to cooperate or a colleague who is unwilling to share resources. As if this conflict is not enough, unrealistic targets, shifting goalposts, and hefty workloads weigh you down. Whatever the case may be, these are all terrible things to have to deal with at work. Luckily, you can change that around and enjoy a more fulfilling working experience. The key to doing this is viewing the situation from a holistic standpoint.

Ask yourself if there is anything you can do to invert the situation and take control over it rather than letting it control you. Often, these three steps prove helpful in resolving workplace conflict and stresses:

- **Develop Self-awareness in the workplace:** Identify what puts your moods off in the workplace. You could feel under pressure or that you don't get along with a colleague, but whatever it may be, it's best to come to terms with it. When you become aware of 'what' or who upsets you, you'll be prepared mentally to try to find a healthy solution to the issue.

- **Practice self-control:** You cannot change other people's actions or unavoidable situations, but you can change how you react towards them. When something upsets you at work, please take a moment to breathe and think of a healthy way to deal with it.
- **Build friendships at work:** Sometimes, having a good friend or two in the workplace can help you look at work through different lenses. This is because having some sort of positive interaction in the workplace can override the negative sentiment that often lingers in it.

As I divulged earlier, I, too, found myself stressed for a very long time in my life; luckily, I was able to escape the hold of stress and live freely again.

### *Breaking the Cycle*

My journey with stress was long and grueling. My mind was constantly clouded by anxious "what ifs" and "if only" as I found myself always stressed out about my work, relationships, and life in general.

I suffered migraines and had a hard time falling asleep at night. And, even when I did manage to get plenty of sleep, it just never seemed enough. I would always wake up in the morning drained.

My life was really unpleasant at the time, and that led me to think if there wasn't a way to change it—and change it for good.

After doing my research on stress management, I soon came to realize that stress will always be a part of life and that stress management is an ongoing process. I identified the things that were responsible for my stress and found ways to counteract them rather than worry endlessly.

I started doing more of the things I found joy in. For example, after a long day of work, I would take a warm bath while listening to my favorite music. I also took time to play with my children as a way to de-stress, and I found that to be really helpful. All of these attempts changed my mood and perception of life.

As a result of making conscious efforts to reduce my stress every day, I finally could say, "Wow, life is not so bad after all..."

Now that we have reached the end of this chapter, I want to let you know that you, too, can break your cycle of stress and live a well-balanced life. It's always crucial to know and understand yourself and your body. What stresses you? What upsets you? What have you come to accept but know doesn't sit well with you? All of these questions will help you to identify your stressors and triggers so you can take the relevant steps to deal with them.

Furthermore, breaking the cycle of stress starts inside your mind. You need to cultivate positivity in order to counteract negativity. And, while it can be challenging to do amidst a whirlwind of stress, it is certainly possible.

Journaling, practicing letting go, and gratitude for all the good in your life are all great for achieving a positive outlook on life.

With that said, exercising regularly, getting enough sleep, and eating healthy can also do wonders in reducing your mounting stress levels. S

ou have taken a massive step, and the results are just around the corner, don't stop now! Come along with me into the next chapter, where we will be talking about building emotional resilience.

# 3

# TIP #1 BUILDING EMOTIONAL RESILIENCE

The oak fought the wind and was broken, the willow bent when it must and survived.

— ROBERT JORDAN

In the world of uncertainty we live in, we cannot stop adversity from taking its course. However, what we can do is to become better prepared for it. This is where resilience comes into play.

Resilience is a key factor in successfully eradicating stress and is the first official tip in your recovery from stress burnout. In this chapter, we will be unpacking all that you need to become more hardy and tough so that stress won't easily knock you over. Essentially, this chapter is centered on creating your line of defense against stress so that you remain in control of your life and not the inverse. Since resilience is all-encompassing, this chapter aims to teach you all the skills and strategies to ultimately grow more resilient. Without waiting any further, let us go straight into it.

## UNDERSTANDING RESILIENCE

Resilience is something we commonly hear about in passing, but with that said, it's usually not paired with a concise definition. In a nutshell, resilience is the ability to bounce back from adversity and recover promptly from tough times. Resilient individuals are more likely to persevere through setbacks and adapt to the ever-changing nature of life. Even when it seems hard to remain positive about life, they can maintain a positive outlook and hope for a better life. What follows is a narrative on Deshawn, whose sense of resilience helped him go through a difficult time.

The COVID-19 pandemic led to an upsurge of stress in many Americans. Dealing with isolation and loss of jobs and loved ones due to illness forced many people to get out of their comfort zones and face adversity head-on. Twenty-five-year-old Deshawn is one such example. After being retrenched from work and losing his mentor, he was distraught and defeated by life. For a period of five months, he found himself unable to focus on anything, let alone get up from his bed.

However, instead of giving into his stress further, he decided to make means to overcome it and, as hard as it was, he came to accept his losses. Although it wasn't something he could necessarily forget about at the snap of a finger, he sought to turn his life into a more positive affair.

Every morning at 7 a.m., Deshawn was up and on his front porch with his journal and a glass of water. He would start by writing down everything he was grateful for in his life, from his family, friends, his home, and his dog Chunks. As he listed all the obvious and big things he was thankful for, even the small, subtle things sprouted in his mind.

He gained cognizance of how lucky he was to even be awake and watching the orange-purple sky at dawn. The more he was grateful, the more he saw the positivity in his life and the more that positivity overpowered the negativity. After feeling down for a long time, his struggles didn't dictate how he lived his life, he was much happier and had better control over his life.

For Deshawn, resilience proved a key component in offsetting his stress. During stressful times, it is important to keep yourself protected from the harmful effects of stress. In the context of trying times, resilience can be seen as a protective shield that will save you from stress's flying spears.

### *Resilience in Stress Management*

Stress brings forth an endless list of physical, psychological, and social issues for those who suffer from it. However, with resilience, mitigating the effects of stress can be made a lot easier.

It allows individuals to view problems objectively and find appropriate solutions to them. Resilient people are equipped with the necessary tools and strategies to negate unfavorable circumstances and turn them into something positive.

As we discussed previously, stress sends us into a prolonged state of "fight-or-flight," which has deleterious health effects. Resilience can help you flip the off switch on this chronically activated stress response mechanism and steer your life in the right direction.

By serving as a buffer from the influx of negative emotions that come with stress, it can improve your overall mood and ability to adapt to challenges.

Through it, you can learn to take better care of your health, solve problems effectively, and even build better relationships than you otherwise would if you were stressed. Moreover, being resilient means you deal with stress in a positive and uplifting way. So, while we can't totally avoid stress, it's always good to know that there are ways of shielding ourselves from it. Usually, the first rule in becoming resilient is being emotionally intelligent. Let's find out more about this.

### Fostering Emotional Intelligence

Although the idea of it has always been a part of human culture, the term emotional intelligence was formally put forth by Dr. Peter Salovey and Dr. John D. Mayer in 1990. Emotional intelligence is the cornerstone of resilience, but what does it really mean? Emotional intelligence refers to the capacity to become fully aware of our emotions and those of the people around us (Cherry, 2023). A great way to look at emotional intelligence is as a compass that helps us navigate our pool of endless emotions. It guides us through the complexities of our emotions and those of other people.

When you are emotionally intelligent, you can understand and manage your feelings, empathize with others, and make informed decisions based on emotion.

In fact, it has been found that people who display emotional intelligence are more equipped to deal with challenges and emerge stronger from them (Collado-

Soler et al., 2023). So, they undeniably work hand in hand. In real life, this is what the link would look like:

Sarah is a project manager at a fast-paced tech company with a reputation for high-quality work. This is not the only value she has to offer to her company. Sarah is also a quintessence of exceptional emotional intelligence.

It happens that, one day, the online project she and her team had been working on for months ran late for submission due to a technical glitch. There is an upheaval in the office, everyone is panicking and stressing their socks off.

Sarah observes the emotional state of her co-workers and decides to call for a team meeting. She asks them to openly divulge what they are feeling and why they are feeling that way—despite the reason being obvious.

Sarah takes the initiative to hear them out, validate their feelings, and show empathy for the situation.

Having listened to all the concerns of the team members, she reassures them that everything will be alright and that they are not alone.

She then sets the mood for an open conversation and a brainstorming session, ensuring that everyone is heard in the process. She empowers her team, shifting their mindset from negative thoughts to positive ones.

This is something she wouldn't have been able to do without emotional intelligence. Instead of freaking out along with her co-workers, Sarah remained calm and in control of her emotions, while also acknowledging those of the people around her.

Furthermore, she came up with a well-thought-out action plan to deal effectively with her team's emotional turmoil and turn it into something good.

As a result of her emotional intelligence, her team regains their motivation and collaborates effectively. Now, her team can function optimally and come up with solutions to their problems.

In the above scenario, Sarah's emotional intelligence played a big role in how she coped with an extremely stressful situation. It made her more resilient and able to take control of the situation rather than letting it control her. Sarah rose to the challenge, displayed exceptional positive problem-solving skills, and remained composed throughout the crisis. This is essentially how emotionally intelligent individuals handle difficult situations.

### *Techniques for Developing Emotional Intelligence*

It's difficult to give your best when your life is in upheaval. However, being emotionally intelligent can make you more resilient and better able to weather the storm.

Being able to tap into and understand your emotions is fundamental in making wise decisions in both good and bad times. In fact, with this bustling work life we are now exposed to, some employers actually seek emotional intelligence as a mandatory requirement in their workers. This is an important life skill for improving productivity and reducing the risk of a perpetual cycle of stress.

Now, the question is as follows: Are we born installed with this component of hardiness, or is it something that we actively have to acquire? The truth is that people are not the same. Others are naturally emotionally intelligent people, while others aren't so great in that department. Every so often, our upbringing and company play a significant role in influencing how emotionally intelligent we become. If you grew up surrounded by people with the characteristic trait, then following the same part becomes easier. Likewise, if you grew up around people who weren't so emotionally intelligent, then that aspect of stress management will remain fairly alien to you. But whatever the case is, there are always things you can do to acquire it or enhance it. Let us take a look at these.

## Start Your Day Off with a Clear Purpose

While we are all used to waking up in panic at what the day ahead has in store, it is always important to slow down and take some time to think. Every day needs a driving force that fuels it. Before getting started with your day, you should always ask yourself what your purpose for the day is. For instance, "I have to keep my cool" or "I have to keep a tunnel vision and focus today." This is great for setting the emotional tone for the day. With the day's purpose clarified, it is easier to start planning how to get about your day.

## Keep Taking Care of Yourself

Just as it is essential to prepare your academic or professional intellect for a big exam or presentation, it is also mandatory to prepare for your emotional intelligence to perform at its best. This can be achieved through taking good care of yourself. Regular exercise, healthy eating, and engaging in mood-boosting activities all put you in the right position to make emotionally intelligent decisions.

## Check Up Regularly on Your Emotions

The complex nature of life can bring forth a wide range of stressors, and to mitigate them successfully, it is important to be aware of the way we respond to them emotionally and physically. Let's say, for instance, physically, your heart is pounding, and your hands are extremely sweaty. And, on the emotional aspect, you might feel anxious or worried. It is always critical to take these stress signals seriously and use them to uncover their possible cause. You could be running late for an important event, or your boss has you bogged down with an endless list of tasks. It literally could be anything. However, the most important thing is making those vital connections that lead you to uncover your stressors and find sensible solutions to them.

## Slow Down

While it may be tempting to react impulsively to a stressful situation, it is always best to slow down, take a deep breath and analyze the situation. Taking a moment to breathe and calm down can help you come up with positive ways to deal with the problem at hand and also prevent you from doing something regrettable.

## Be Willing to Share All Kinds of Emotions, Not Only the Pleasant Ones

A common trait of an emotionally intelligent person is vulnerability. When you are emotionally intelligent, you are not afraid to ask for help or advice when it is needed. This, however, is not the same as airing your dirty laundry and shouldn't be confused with doing so. Instead, it is a survival tactic that can be used to garner help and moral support in dire times, helping to lighten your load and reduce your stress.

For effective stress management, emotional intelligence is applicable in everyday life. More than we like it, we are bound to encounter a situation that shakes us up emotionally. It is just an inevitable part of life.

What's great is that, with emotional intelligence, you no longer have to fall victim to the grueling effect of stress. You can deal with and eliminate stressors as they come, rather than letting them pile up and become insurmountable.

We have talked all about emotional intellect and the role it plays in making us more resilient and, ultimately, in stress management. Let us now explore how acceptance and adaptability can help you to become resilient and keep stress at bay.

### *How Does Acceptance Lead to Resilience*

Acceptance is often followed by negative connotations such as "forfeiting issues rather than facing them head-on," cowardice, and weakness. In actual fact, the opposite is true. Acceptance is a gateway to becoming mentally tough and resilient.

Resilience is the ability to overcome life challenges and prepare us against adversity. On the other hand, acceptance can be defined as the readiness to come to terms with life and its occurrences. These two factors can greatly influence your outlook on life and how you handle challenges.

In fact, to paint a vivid picture of the link between acceptance and resilience, psychologists have come up with a term that describes the inability to accept—negative willfulness.

Acceptance is a game changer when it comes to being resilient and dealing with hardship in general. When you open yourself up to accepting life for what it really is, you bolster your ability to deal with challenges effectively.

Acceptance means not resorting to the blame game or being avoidant when things get tough.

While it can be tempting to reallocate the blame for our shortcomings and failures to other people, it is always important to view ourselves as a part of the picture. The simple act of doing this puts you in control as the driver or the main determining factor of your life, rather than a 'passenger'. This way, you will accept responsibility for your life and focus your efforts on changing its course.

Resilience arises when you opt to accept problems instead of avoiding them. It prepares you mentally to fight the problem, making you more confident that you are capable of circumventing it.

Learning to accept can take you a long way in terms of dealing with stress. However, it isn't something that is built-in, and for that reason, we should always work towards being more accepting.

### How to Embrace and Accept Change in Order to Manage Stress

Stress is a direct result of change, particularly the negative kind. While we can instantaneously accept good changes, such as getting a new car or a new house, it is always harder to come to terms with bad changes. For example, getting a sudden influx of work or bankruptcy can be significantly more difficult changes to embrace. However, as tough as it is to accept and embrace change in our lives, it is certainly not impossible. Let us look at some strategies you can use to make change easier to assimilate into and embrace.

## Analyze the Possibilities

Change looks terrible from the outset, but there is more to it than just negativity. Whenever you are faced with any sort of change that interferes with your normal way of life, it is always important to be objective. This means analyzing both good and bad outcomes that may come along. By doing this, you will realize that change is not all that bad after all. Let's take the example of having to relocate because of a new job. This might interfere with the convenience you get from living in an area that you have already gotten used to. However, if you flipped the coin, you'd realize that the change does bring some sort of positivity. Moving could be a great way to learn to get out of your comfort zone and to meet new people.

## Keep On Updating Your Coping Mechanism

As seasons change, the phases of our lives also change. It is critical for us to keep up to date with these changes by devising adaptive coping methods. One situation may call for you to whip out your time management skills, like working in a high-paced industry. Another situation may call on you to practice patience and mindfulness, all as a way of adapting to change. So, with that being said, it's always indispensable to analyze the change and match it with relevant coping mechanisms.

## Reframe Your Mindset

Undoubtedly, change is difficult to make peace with, but changing your perception of it can really make a difference. When change arises, take a moment to feel whatever emotions it evokes in you, understand why you feel that way, and work towards changing your thoughts into positive ones.

Change is all around us and is present for the greater part of our lives. Some changes are big and drastic, and others are small and harder to notice; however, no matter the magnitude of change, these tools will always help you to accept it, grow through it, and eventually overcome it. However, accepting and embracing change also works hand-in-hand with having a growth mindset. Let us look further into this.

### *Fostering a Growth Mindset*

It is widely accepted that people are not the same. The same goes for the way we perceive life and its challenges in general. In most cases, an individual either has a fixed mindset or a growth mindset. The difference in these two types of mindsets is one of the factors that can greatly influence a person's susceptibility to stress.

A fixed mindset is one that holds the sentiment that we are all born with a fixed set of skills. It's either we can do something, or we can't, and there isn't much we can do to change that. Conversely, a growth mindset is one that seeks to expand and explore the world of possibility.

People with a growth mindset hardly succumb to a challenge. Instead, they find all means to equip themselves with the skills they need to elude the predicament. Unlike those with a fixed mindset, people with a growth mindset take obstacles as learning curves and opportunities to grow. This is an essential skill in stress management because when you look at challenges through the lens of positivity, you alleviate the worry and fears that string along. You, instead, instill in yourself the confidence that you can grow through whatever you face and overcome your challenges. Here are some pointers for transforming a fixed mindset into a growth mindset.

From everything we have discussed in this chapter, it can be deduced that resilience is the combination of emotional intelligence, acceptance, and a growth mindset.

In terms of being resilient, one cannot exist without the other. To successfully deal with stress, it is important to make each of them a normal part of your daily life. Eventually, you will see and feel a load of stress being lifted from your shoulders.

As we briefly discussed in the earlier chapters, there are many ways to recognize the onset of stress burnout. Dealing with stress from the get-go is a prerogative as it allows you to deal with problems as soon as they surface instead of letting them pile up.

This is the topic of the next chapter. We will be learning all about spotting the warning signs of stress and finding ways to reverse them effectively.

# 4

# TIP #2: RECOGNIZING THE RED FLAGS AND WARNING SIGNS

A 2009 study on a group of 587 working-class individuals found that 59% of them suffered mild and severe stress. According to the study, this stress likely puts them at risk of suffering burnout and a range of mental illnesses such as depression and anxiety (Wiegner et al., 2015).

This leaves us to wonder just how much the prevalence of stress has increased among most populations almost 14 years later. Technological improvements, new and demanding work expectations, and the general rat race of the modern day all contribute to that stress.

While we cannot necessarily run away from all that, it is vital to always shield ourselves against it. And knowing all the red flags and warning signs is a great way to do that.

Being aware of the signs of stress burnout can help you seek help to find ways to deal with it better. I understand that some people aren't actually aware that they are stressed, and this can have damaging effects.

This is why this chapter is centered around recognizing all the red flags and warning signs of stress, which is the second official tip of the book. By the end of this chapter, you will know everything you need to know about what stresses you the most and how to keep it on the curb. Let's delve right into it.

## THE PHYSICAL SYMPTOMS OF STRESS

One major issue is that you can live with stress without actually seeing the red flags. You might find yourself dragging on and on, only to find out after some time that you are suffering from stress. That was precisely what happened to me.

I felt like a car driving on an empty tank. I had no energy to keep me going or keep me focused on my personal and work life, but I kept going. My days were riddled with an overwhelming sense of fatigue, headaches, muscle aches, and panic attacks. But through all those warning signs, I never thought I was stressed. Each time I felt like that, I simply blamed myself for being lazy and finding excuses not to work.

So, with that, I was harsh on myself and pushed myself harder. I thought this would get rid of all the feelings that plagued me, but it didn't. It only led me to feel worse.

My heart would randomly start beating out of my chest, and my whole body would break out in sweat. In addition to that, I suffered from persistent headaches, and no matter how much I tried to stay hydrated, they just wouldn't go away.

Living like that was really getting the best of me and getting in my way of living a normal life. I couldn't spend time with my family and participate in my favorite hobbies.

I no longer enjoyed activities that I used to, and whenever someone asked me to do something, I came up with an excuse as to why I couldn't.

Eventually, I came to realize that something was terribly wrong with me and sought a doctor's help.

She told me that everything I had been experiencing was a direct result of stress, and from that day I vouched never to be oblivious to any indication of stress.

For most people, it's only after a breaking point that they see that they have been chronically stressed. However, dealing with full-blown stress is much more challenging. This is because, by that time, the chances of you having acquired a stress-related illness are high.

The great news is that you don't have to wait until something terrible happens. You can prevent that from happening right here and right now. The following is a checklist (not a self-diagnosis) to help you learn whether you are suffering from stress or not:

| | |
|---|---|
| Headaches | Chest pain/tightness |
| Muscle tension | Weakened immune system |
| Fatigue | Restlessness |
| Sleep disturbances | Skin problems |
| Increased heart rate | Nausea/ upset stomach |
| Digestive issues | Dizziness |
| Changes in appetite | Shallow breathing |

If you find that you display the majority of these symptoms, then that could be an indication that you are stressed out.

When you are stressed out, it is evident that your mental state is in upheaval: you may find that you just lost your wallet, you forgot to pick up your children from school, or your brain is going through an influx of worrying thoughts that are driving you nuts.

As we learned earlier, stress affects each part of our body, including our mental health.

### Mental and Mood Indicators

Stress can either be acute or chronic. The difference between the two is what determines the extent to which the latter is toxic for your health. Acute stress is momentary and likely to dissipate within a short space of time. It can sharpen your focus and help you to react promptly to a problem at a given moment. However, when that stress doesn't wear off, this can adversely impact various aspects of your health, including your cognitive well-being.

In simple terms, your cognitive well-being is the capacity of your brain to concentrate or orchestrate tasks. These can range from simple activities such as switching on the house alarm at night to more complex undertakings like mental alertness during a high-stakes exam.

When you are chronically stressed, your cognitive functioning takes strain. This is because your body directs energy preserved for cognitive activities to other parts of the body to fight off the perceived threat or stressor. Consequently, your brain is left with very little energy to function optimally. It is important to be on the lookout for the red flags of stress in your cognitive functioning, as this will help you to seek help. The following are some of the biggest and most prevalent cognitive impairments caused by stress.

## Forgetfulness or Memory Loss

Research has shown that stress can cause a regression in our ability to remember things (Marais, 2022). This can be both in the long and short term. When you are stressed, your mind's ability to absorb and retain information decreases drastically. This can lead you to forget too often or even misremember the sequence of events.

## Impaired Concentration

When your mind is clouded with problems and worries, it is hard to focus on what is at hand. You may even find your concentration going south during an important meeting or while you are trying to focus on reaching a looming work deadline. This can be highly frustrating and can also put you at further risk of becoming more stressed. All of that can negatively impact your work performance and quality of life in general.

## Constant Worrying

Stress can have you worrying all day and every day. Even when you try not to, your mind will be plagued by constant what-ifs and an intense feeling of impending doom. You will feel like, regardless of what you try to do, things won't be okay. This can also back up the point made above, as you might find yourself worrying more than focusing on completing a task.

## Poor Judgment

Stress is a driver of impulsivity. All too often, you can find yourself making poorly thought-out decisions, even when it isn't necessarily your nature. In fact, to prove this, a study conducted in 2012 demonstrated that those who suffer from chronic stress are more likely to act impulsively than those who are less stressed (Marais, 2022).

But, while these cognitive impairments may stand out in our daily lives, these aren't the only effects of stress on the mind. Just like you did with the physical symptoms of stress, you can use the following checklist of red flags to determine the extent to which stress is affecting your cognitive well-being.

| | |
|---|---|
| Anxiety | Rumination |
| Irritability | Low self-esteem |
| Mood Swings | Feelings of hopelessness |
| Racing thoughts | Overthinking |
| Negative self-talk | |
| Difficulty making decisions | |
| Feeling overwhelmed | |
| Panic attacks | |

If you find that you experience most of the above symptoms, then it is a big indicator that your stress is taking a toll on your mental and cognitive health. Don't worry; there are plenty of solutions to that.

### Coping With Mental Stress

It is a well-accepted fact that life is inherently stressful, but that doesn't mean it always has to be that way. Let us look at some tips to improve your mental health and get a step ahead of stress.

### Value Yourself

Just as much as you prioritize taking care of work and other personal obligations, it is also important that you put yourself first. Always respect yourself, treat yourself with kindness, and avoid being overly critical of yourself. You can also engage in hobbies, like listening to your favorite music, beautifying your home garden, or playing a chess game with a friend.

## Take Care of Yourself

A very vital aspect of ameliorating mental stress is taking care of yourself—physically. This includes eating wholesome and well-balanced meals, avoiding unhealthy habits such as smoking, getting an adequate amount of sleep, and spending enough time outdoors exercising, particularly in the sun.

## Surround Yourself with Positive-Minded People

Link up with people who share multiple strong familial and friendship bonds. These types of people usually have greater communication skills, and since they hold a sense of togetherness and inclusivity, they are more capable of uplifting those around them.

## Break the Monotony

There is always a sense of comfort in following a routine. But, sometimes, this routine can also be a source of dullness and ultimately an addition to your stress. This is because stressors are often embedded in routine, and breaking that cycle can help reduce your stress level.

Stress is like a vine that invades a garden, wrapping itself around every aspect of our lives and choking out all the joy that once flourished freely. One of these aspects is our behavior in day-to-day occurrences.

### Behavioral Warning Signs

During his college years, Tevin was known as a bubbly personality who got along with all kinds of people. Even the most difficult people couldn't resist his charm, as he instantly filled the room with smiles. However, after college, what used to be a people person changed completely.

Although Tevin was a qualified electrical engineer, he struggled to find employment. Because of his financial state, he couldn't pay his bills or get much done, and this caused him a great deal of stress. He was drowning in the pressures of adult life and changing in ways no one had ever thought possible.

Tevin developed an inferiority complex, which decreased his self-esteem and made him reluctant to mix and mingle with others. His social withdrawal burned bridges between him and other members of his previously solid social circles.

Tevin just wanted to be left alone, and anyone who tempered with his peace would be received by a mouthful of unwelcoming words. He was often cranky and would lash out, with or without reason. The Tevin he once was had thoroughly changed, and it was all because of stress.

It's a sad reality, but stress burnout can change people in ways unimaginable. It can alter the parts of our brains that are responsible for controlling our behaviors, leading to wayward actions. Just as it is important to know your emotional and mental reactions to stress, it is equally critical to recognize your behavioral patterns. This is so that we can find ways to counteract them. The following table will help you to know how stress affects your behavior.

| | |
|---|---|
| Changes in eating habits | Avoidance of responsibilities |
| Procrastination | Nail biting or fidgeting |
| Escapism (excessive or obsessive behaviors such as playing too many video games and substance abuse) | Social withdrawal |
| Changes in communication patterns | Decreased interest activities |
| Overworking/perfectionism | Outbursts of anger |
| Neglecting self-care | Impulsive behaviors |

No matter how many of the above symptoms you experience, there are always solutions to help reduce them.

***Strategies to Address Stress-Driven Behavior and Their Triggers***

All too often, we find ourselves being controlled by the strings of stress as if we are puppets. As we start acting according to our stressors, our behavior changes, and it is as if we turn into an entirely new being. But there are many ways you can keep your behavior in check and deal with your stress-driven behaviors. The following are some great ways to do this.

- **Self-awareness:** Dealing with only the result of a stressor is ineffective, but what isn't is dealing with the stressor itself. It is important to become aware of the reason behind the way you behave, as this will lead you in the right direction.
- **Form healthy habits:** The negative behavioral response that is caused by stress usually goes hand in hand with bad habits. Breaking these habits and repetitive cycles is imperative when handling stress-driven behaviors. The best way to do this is to replace bad habits like binge eating and inactivity with healthier exercising and nutritious dieting.

- **Positive reinforcement:** Take note of all the efforts you make to behave in a healthier manner and reward yourself for them.
- **Emotional regulation:** Stress-driven behaviors are directly linked to poor emotional regulation. When you are stressed, it is always a good choice to take time to analyze your emotions and regulate them accordingly. Deep breathing is a great way to calm and recollect yourself during tumultuous times.

Sometimes, the manner in which we behave when we are cornered by stress can have ripple effects on our lives, affecting ourselves and the people around us. For this reason, it is often advisable to take actionable steps to prevent this from happening.

When we don't understand how stress impacts us, we are inclined to normalize certain behaviors and harmful stress-related symptoms. The sole purpose of this chapter was to educate you on all the ways that stress can affect you.

I hope that you are now fully aware of what stress does to your body, mind, and behavior. Knowing this makes a huge difference in how you will deal with stress from now on and is a considerable leap in your journey to recovery.

Among the many ways there are to deal with stress, mindfulness, and meditation are one of the buzzing topics. This is our topic in the next chapter, so get ready to move into chapter 5, where the world of mindfulness and meditation awaits!

# 5

# TIP #3: MINDFULNESS AND MEDITATION

The subtle art of being mindful has been largely associated with lower levels of stress (Wein, 2021). Practicing mindfulness can help open your mind to new possibilities and dimensions of life, and in doing so, it provides excellent tools for dealing with the stress of daily life. Because our stressors are usually embedded in many aspects of our lives, you must employ mindfulness and meditation in everything you do. When you learn to do this, your reality will be less stressful. This chapter is a walkthrough of everything you need to know about mindfulness and meditation and how they can relieve you of stress. By the end of the chapter, you will know what it really means to be mindful, as well as how you can make it your greatest weapon in the battle against stress.

## WHAT DOES IT MEAN TO BE MINDFUL?

In life, you can either have your mind full or be mindful. This sounds complex, but there is definitely a lot of sense behind this.

When your mind is full, it runs a production of thoughts on the past or on what the future is likely to hold. However, this prevents you from living in the moment and from dealing with what is at stake at that given time. Conversely, when you are mindful, your mind is in the now. You focus on the present moment with nothing but an open and nonjudgmental outlook. Since our problems and worries are usually rooted in "what could have been" and in "what might be," being mindful is a great way to escape the negativity of those thoughts.

And, while we are born with an innate probability to be mindful, it doesn't reveal itself unless we intentionally make an effort for it to happen. Precisely put, mindfulness is not something that happens; it is an art that requires mastery. To achieve a mindful state, you need to frequently train your mind to be comfortable in living in the here and now.

With the booming stress levels among millennials, mindfulness has attracted a lot of popularity as a go-to stress relief method. The following is a story of how

Cristine broke free from the clench of stress through mindfulness.

Twenty-five-year-old Cristine has had a bad bout of stressful life events over the last few months. Her personal and work life has been in total upheaval, and she is struggling to juggle her responsibilities all at once. Workwise, she has looming deadlines that make her overwork herself. In her personal life, she is a mother of a two-year-old son and a caregiver for her sick mother.

Including her needs, all these aspects of her life constantly vie for her undivided attention and are quite honestly spreading her thinness. However, after coming across an article that explained mindfulness, her life has changed from what it was. She now worries less about the past and the future. Instead, focuses her attention on the present moment and what she can do to maximize it.

Being mindful has allowed her to deal with her previously high stress levels, and because she lives in the moment, she has full control over her life.

To truly be mindful, there are specific characteristic traits that you need to acquire. Mindfulness consists of seven principles, each one playing a unique role in instilling an unshakable sense of mindfulness.

### *The Seven Fundamentals of Mindfulness*

The following are the characteristic traits that make a mindful being.

- **Non-judging:** Avoid any temptations to judge or alter your experiences. This also means that you separate yourself from what you go through in life.
- **Patience:** This is the beauty of knowing that things only happen when the timing is right.
- **Beginner's mind:** A beginner's mind can be likened to that of a child in the earliest developmental phase—curious and willing to learn more. This is something that mindfulness calls for.
- **Trust:** Gain trust in yourself, your capability, and your ability to overcome. This also means trusting the process in anything you do.
- **Non-striving:** Appreciate the simplicity of the moment you are in. Take everything as it comes and avoid changing anything.
- **Acceptance:** Understanding that what is done is done and there is no turning back.
- **Letting go:** We all have the tendency to dwell on our experiences. It is important to stop overthinking and to let go.

Mindfulness is a combination of all these things. There are many ways that you can practice mindfulness and relinquish your stress. The following are some well-known methods of mindfulness.

### Body Scan Meditation

With everything going on around us, it can be difficult to establish a true body-mind connection. What this means is that you get to understand every feeling, tension, and sensation that runs through your body and how it is connected to your mental state. Body scan meditation is a great way to do this, particularly because it allows you to understand everything that is going on in your body fully. It is basically using your mind to perform a detailed analysis of your body. By doing so, you tune into the present moment, taking note of everything in the now. This is how you can do it:

- Start in a sitting position, inhale through your nose, and then exhale through your mouth.
- Using your mind, start scanning your body from the very top of your head all the way to your toes, or vice versa.
- While doing this, be sure to pay attention to all the sensations, tensions, and emotions that are

running through each part of your body as you
scan it.

- Bear in mind that this is not about judging the
  moment or anything that your body feels.
  Rather, it is simply about immersing yourself in
  the moment and being one with it.

### Breath Awareness

A good way to divert from a stressful situation is to focus on your breath. Concentrating on your breath-work can be a valuable weapon in fighting against stress and other stress-related problems such as anxiety, depression, and pain. This is because it can serve as a focal point for us to control how we behave and react when we are stressed. Furthermore, there are many opportunities that can be exploited to work on breath work. You can take note of your breathing patterns when you are happy, sad, worried, and even when you are excited—anytime is a good time to do this.

### Sensory Awareness

A crucial component of mindfulness is being observant. In mindfulness terms, this refers to the ability to connect your body and mind to your surroundings using your senses. Your five senses are a gateway to mental, physical, and spiritual alignment. This is because they fully bring you into the present moment, allowing for any thoughts, experiences, and pains to dissolve as your focus shifts towards the now. Engaging with your senses slows down stressful thoughts and instead helps you to truly enjoy the beauty of the moment at hand. This mindfulness strategy is extremely calming to both the mind and the body; furthermore, it is easy to indulge in; all you need is your five senses and a tranquil setting to perform it. As there are five senses to our sensory ability, this mindfulness practice also has five parts to it. The following are directions on how to do them.

- Begin in a seated position, with your hands placed comfortably on top of your thighs. Take a moment to recollect yourself from the events of your hectic day, and then once you are calm, take a deep, slow, and controlled breath.
- Once you've done this, shift your attention from your breath to the sounds in your vicinity. The first sounds that should meet your ears are the loudest and most pervasive ones, for example, a baby crying or a tree feller cutting down the neighbor's tree. Not all sounds will be pleasant but keep trusting the process. As you settle in and fully exploit your sense of hearing, you should be able to notice the subtle sounds you didn't hear initially.

- Once you are done with that, shift your focus to the sense of smell. Imagine that your nose is a massive vacuum that draws in all sorts of smells as you pick up all the surrounding scents, both pleasant and unpleasant. You might smell a pot of chili sauce being cooked somewhere or maybe the fabric softener you used for your linen. Whatever it may be, allow your sense of smell to gain cognizance of it.

- Open your eyes in case you had closed them in the previous steps. This is because the next exercise needs you to engage your sense of sight. Look around you, and without much intention, take note of all the things you see. Pay attention to how each object differs in color, shape, and size from the next.

- Once you are done with that, the next step is to concentrate on your sense of taste. This step can be performed with or without food, depending on whether you have any available. If you don't have food, simply focus on what your mouth tastes. This could be just the natural taste of your mouth, the taste of the lamb chops that you had for lunch, or the soda you just had 10 minutes ago. However, if food is available to you, you can just do this exercise like you did in the previous steps. Take note of all the different tastes, textures, and shapes of the foods you are consuming.

- Finally, the last step is to focus on your sense of touch. While you are seated, take note of how you relate to your environment. How does the chair or the ground beneath you feel? How do your clothes feel on you? Are they tight, or are they loose? Where are your hands placed, and how does it feel? Is it rough, smooth, or is it ribbed? Be sure to pay attention to all these things without trying to change them in any way.

- Once you have completed all the steps above, you can gently get up from your seated position. As you do this, notice how much calmer both your mind and body are than before. You should feel like a load has been lifted off your shoulders and ready to take on life in the context of the present.

### *Benefits of Mindfulness for Stress*

Mindfulness practices aren't just a temporary fix for stress. The results of mindfulness are perpetual, helping you to shield yourself from stress anytime it prevails. As you make it a habitual practice, you will notice that dedicating just five minutes of your day to mindfulness can really go a long way. Below are some benefits.

- **Stress Reduction:** Mindfulness helps lower stress by promoting relaxation and reducing the body's stress response.
- **Cognitive Flexibility:** It fosters adaptability and flexible thinking, enabling better problem-solving.
- **Enhanced Relaxation:** Mindfulness techniques induce relaxation responses that counter stress-induced tension.

Understandably so, you may worry about having spare time to squeeze mindfulness into your already busy schedule. However, this might not necessarily be a problem because there are many ways to incorporate mindfulness into your day.

*Integrating Mindfulness into Daily Life*

Reaping the benefits of mindfulness doesn't require that you spend hours and hours on end engaging in it. You may be busy, but surely, there is an extra five minutes that you can put aside for some meditation. You might already have an idea of when that time could be, but if you don't, here are some perfect moments to sneak mindfulness into your day.

- **Practice first thing in the morning:** Since you might get busier as the day goes on, take the initiative to start your day off with a mindful moment.

- **Mindful eating:** Have your meals in a distraction-free area, where you will be able to focus on them without random interruptions.
- **Breathing breaks:** Regardless of where you are, you can always pause to take a few mindful breaks. This can be after a hectic work meeting or even during a hectic work schedule.
- **Waiting time:** We all get frustrated by having to wait, especially when our time doesn't allow it. So, why not turn these waiting periods into something more beneficial? Whether you are waiting for a call center agent to attend to your call or waiting to get served your takeaway, take those moments to be mindful. Sensory awareness is best for this kind of situation.
- **Night reflection:** If your mornings are all too hectic for you to get a mindful moment out, then just before best might be a viable alternative. Take a few minutes before bed to close your eyes and reflect on the good that happened in your day and anything that you are grateful for.

These are just some ways to incorporate mindfulness into your day; however, the list goes on. Study your daily patterns and see if there are other small time slots you can designate for meditation.

We have come to the end of this chapter, and I hope that you now have a broad knowledge of what mindfulness is. The most important thing to do when it comes to being mindful is to trust the process and focus on what is immediate to you. In doing so, you automatically let go of all the negative sentiments which are linked to the thoughts of the past and future.

Another significant aspect of your journey to recovery is learning to set boundaries around your thoughts, emotions, and personal space. That, precisely, is what we will be discussing in the next chapter. So, let us get right into it.

# 6

## TIP #4: SETTING BOUNDARIES AND PRIORITIZING SELF-CARE

When was the last time you did what you love, or let alone had a moment to relax and listen to the inner you? Currently, this is a question that many people struggle to produce an actual answer to. We spend so much time focusing on doing things for other people that we forsake our well-being. But, if you are truly to set yourself free from the burden of stress, re-evaluating your boundaries and self-care is imperative.

This brings us to the fourth official tip of the book and one that will help you cope even during the most stressful times. In this chapter, we will be shedding light on the importance of setting clear and realistic boundaries to protect your well-being, while still attending to the matters of life. Towards the end of this chapter, you will have a newfound perception of what setting boundaries and self-care actually mean. Finally, with the practical steps at your disposal, you will be able to translate that knowledge into your life.

## THE IMPORTANCE OF SELF-CARE

It may not be apparent from the outset, but neglecting yourself can really take a toll on your self-esteem and confidence. This is because constantly overlooking the basic human need of taking care of oneself and setting healthy boundaries makes you feel less important. Furthermore, when you don't do things to uplift, reset, and protect yourself, you put yourself in a position where you are more susceptible to stress.

The following is a story about Janette, whose self-neglect spiraled out of control.

Janette is many things, but those who know her well would say she is passionate and full of fire. In fact, one could even say she is Superwoman material. Working two jobs and being a mother, wife, sister, daughter, and friend are all duties that she constantly has to fulfill. However, beneath that juggling act is a woman under immense pressure to conform so much so that she has totally forgotten about herself.

After traveling twice to and from America and Australia for work-related conferences and meetings, she has never felt so unfamiliar with herself. She rarely has any time available to take care of herself and to do the things she loves. Moreover, because she puts on a tough facade, she is constantly attending to other people's requests, forgetting about her own.

Everything that once defined her is slowly diminishing from her life. She can't even watch her favorite series anymore, let alone get some quiet time to herself.

The result of her self-neglect has been an ongoing mental and emotional breakdown. At times, it is so bad that she is unable to get out of her bed. Because of a lack of self-care and boundaries, what once was a joyful life turned into a miserable reality.

With meetings to attend, calls to make, and many other matters of life, taking care of oneself can fall to the very bottom of the list of priorities. Besides this, there are misconceptions that cloud the idea of self-care.

### *Cleaning Up Self-Care Misconceptions*

While self-care is a necessity, society hasn't quite understood it well. What people picture it to be isn't what it is. In fact, this misconception has come with a hefty price to pay. It is the reason many people constantly feel spent and why we feel like we don't have control over our lives.

For as long as these misconceptions live, we will never experience what it truly means to be happy. So, without further delay, let us debunk the myth that exists around self-care and relish in what the essence of self-love truly has to offer.

## Myth #1: Self-Care Is Selfish

**Fact:** Many people view the concept of taking time off to focus on yourself as selfishness. The truth is that self-care isn't selfish; it is a vital aspect of maintaining your overall health. Not only will it benefit you, but the people around you. Because when you are well taken care of, your cup overflows with love and positivity.

## Myth #2: Self-care Requires a Lot of Time

**Fact:** Never mind what you've heard about self-care being a lengthy process. It is the far opposite of that. Self-care can be quick and straightforward and doesn't require excessive amounts of energy. Simple acts like taking a short walk or engaging in a brief deep breathing session are more than enough.

## Myth #3: It's Only About Pampering

**Fact:** Pampering is a form of self-care, but not all there is to it. Unlike pampering, which only targets the physical aspects of self-care, self-care is an umbrella term that describes taking care of yourself from an all-round perspective. It is all-encompassing, taking care of your mental, emotional, spiritual, and physical health altogether.

## Myth #4: It's Expensive

**Fact:** While self-care has a stretch of benefits to offer, it definitely won't stretch your pockets. Self-care doesn't have to cost a dime. There are many activities, such as reading and hiking, that can be explored free of cost.

## Myth #5: It's Only for Stressful Times

**Fact:** Self-care should be habitual and not sporadic. Regularly keeping your overall health in check serves as a preventative measure against stress and burnout.

## Myth #6: It's a One-Size-Fits-All Approach

**Fact:** Self-care doesn't look the same for everyone. Some people view self-care as hitting the gym and keeping fit, while others view it as taking time to relax and reflect on their day. It is essential to find your personalized version of self-care.

## Myth #7: It's About Ignoring Responsibility

**Fact:** In no way is taking care of yourself a sign of irresponsibility. It is an essential part of being a whole and healthy being that cannot be overlooked. Furthermore, taking good care of yourself can help improve your focus and provide you with the energy you need to fulfill your responsibilities.

## Myth #8: It's Always a Solo Activity

**Fact:** Sitting in solitude, sipping hot chocolate, and looking into the horizon perfectly epitomizes self-care. But you don't necessarily have to be alone to practice self-care. Spending time with loved ones, engaging in group activities, and seeking support are all forms of self-care, which include the company of others.

The world we live in is full of different opinions and perceptions. Some of which may hinder our progress in leading more stress-free lives. This is why it is important to separate fact from myth.

Now that you know what self-care is and what it isn't, you can start doing more for yourself and reduce your stress levels.

### *Types of Self-Care*

Looking after yourself doesn't mean you need to bend over backward. In fact, somewhere in the corners of your busy day lay many chances for you to practice self-care. You can begin making actionable steps to ensure you are well taken care of right here and right now. Here are some ways you can squeeze this healthy habit into your life and alleviate your stress.

- **Shift your expectations:** While expectations set targets for us to be at par with what we want to accomplish, they can also be damaging in times of stress. Be understanding and patient with yourself in challenging times. Lower your expectations and bear in mind that you can't always be perfect. This, on its own, is a great way to take care of yourself.

- **Take care of your body:** Do you usually rush your showers so that you can proceed with the day's tasks? Or maybe you have been postponing that workout session because of life's demands? Well, if that's the case, slow down and pay more attention to that body. The amount of care you give your body matters in keeping your stress at bay. Be sure to keep yourself clean, nourished, hydrated, and active.

- **Fall back on the activities you love:** What did you love doing that made you so happy? This can be something as small as taking a simple walk or even cooking with your spouse. Whatever that is, start doing it again and bring that happiness and sense of fulfillment back into your life.

- **Laugh, laugh, and laugh:** A good laugh can change the narrative of a bad day into a good one. Spending time with jovial, light-hearted, and entertaining people or putting on your favorite comedy show are all good ways to solicit a good laugh.

Make efforts to incorporate these aspects of self-care into your day, and you'll be sure to see the improvements. But, with that said, remember to keep it personalized to your individual needs.

### Establishing Healthy Boundaries

Setting clear and healthy boundaries is crucial not only for our physical space but also for protecting ourselves from mentally and emotionally taxing situations.

However, establishing boundaries isn't always the easiest thing. It may seem abrupt to all of a sudden wake-up and tell people that you won't be doing something anymore, but it's necessary. Boundaries are a great way to minimize stressful situations and gain a better sense of direction in life.

In essence, healthy boundaries can help us in many ways that we can't imagine. They give you the room to live free of disappointment, unrealistic expectations, and many other issues. Let us briefly look at some things you can expect from setting healthy boundaries.

- **Strengthened relationships:** It may seem like sweeping things under the carpet is the easiest way to avoid conflict; however, it does the opposite. Not being stern about your boundaries can make you feel insignificant and possibly make you hold animosity against others. Conversely, when you are open about what you can tolerate and what you can't, you enable people to act in a way that doesn't make you feel uncomfortable.

- **Improved self-esteem:** The more precise you are on what your boundaries are, the less you will feel taken advantage of, and the greater your self-esteem will be.

- **Avoid burnout:** Burnout is largely a result of unclear or unhealthy boundaries. This is because people tend to neglect and overwork themselves to please others. However, when boundaries are set, it becomes easier for one to help others without depleting their energy reserves.

- **An improved sense of identity:** Nothing speaks louder to a person's soul than knowing themselves thoroughly. Healthy boundaries help you to get a broadened understanding of who you are and what your purpose is.

You have been too nice for too long, and it's time to change that by setting some straightforward boundaries. But where do you start? How do you do it? You can find the answer to that within the following paragraphs.

## SETTING BOUNDARIES PERSONALLY AND PROFESSIONALLY

Stress will always be an inevitable part of life, but knowing when to put a stop to certain things can really help reduce it. Most of our stress stems from not being stern on our boundaries. Be it in your professional or personal life; you need to have a set of no-go zones to protect your well-being. If this is not done, you run the risk of spreading yourself thin and eventually burning out. Let us begin with setting boundaries in the workplace.

### *How to Set Boundaries in the Workplace*

Everything in life works well when there are boundaries in place. Before going further, let us clarify why it is important to establish boundaries in the working environment.

A healthy set of boundaries can help you keep your work-life balance in check. Without them, our work life and home life would merge, making it hard for us to control our lives. This can have a negative impact on your mental health, leading to high levels of stress. However, these aren't the only benefits, and the list goes on. The following are some of the many benefits of setting boundaries in the workplace.

- **Increased productivity:** Setting boundaries helps you to divert distractions at work and reduce the likelihood of burning out. This can make you work more productively.
- **Keeps workload manageable:** Governing the number of 'healthy' hours you can work each day and taking on a reasonable number of tasks at a time can help you manage your workload.
- **Improves your job satisfaction and collaborative energy:** Chances of you enjoying your job are high when it isn't weighing heavy on you.

Now that you know of all the benefits, here are some tips you can apply in the workplace to ensure healthy boundaries.

- **Set priorities:** List all your work obligations in order from top priority to last priority. Usually, a good take on this would be to establish this order based on what is time-sensitive and important, urgent but not important, important but not urgent, and lastly, not urgent and not important.

- **Delegate tasks:** When your plate gets a little too full, there is always someone who can help you take care of a task or maybe even be better qualified to do it. However, to avoid conflicts, always consult your manager or supervisor beforehand.

- **Take a break:** When you feel the need to take a break, do so. You may also want to inquire if your company offers personal paid leave so that you can take time off to readjust yourself. Likewise, if you are unwell, don't force yourself to work; take a day off to recover.

- **Get comfortable saying 'no':** Giving 'no' for an answer is an art that takes time to master. Most of us feel bad for saying no to the requests of other people. We feel like we are letting them down or as if we aren't reliable. Some of us may even feel like failures. However, this isn't remotely the case.

Likewise, it is important to apply the same principles to your personal life. Setting boundaries in your personal life will help you manage how you relate to yourself and others much better. Furthermore, it will help get rid of unnecessary stressors.

### How to Set Boundaries in Your Personal Life

Do you ever feel like people always get their way with you (even your loved ones)? Or, maybe you feel like you need to speak up more? We all feel like that at some point in our lives, and this can cause strain on our mental and emotional well-being.

Safeguarding your mental and emotional health is an important step towards thriving in your personal life. Here is how you can do this:

- **Make time for yourself:** Whether you are an extrovert or an introvert, you need to put aside time to be alone and away from others—even your spouse.
- **Put a stop to toxic codependency:** Though we love and care for our friends and family, there are some who take advantage of this. Some may constantly ask you for money, while others may ask you for favors that make you feel uncomfortable. Whatever it is, be sure to put a stop to it.
- **Protect your time:** Don't feel bad about turning down a request from a loved one if your time isn't so flexible. If they love you, they

will truly understand that you get caught up at times.

Remember that setting boundaries doesn't particularly imply that you have to be rude. Boundaries can be set politely without hurting or offending other people.

When setting boundaries, it is important to do so in a polite tone, as this ensures that no hard feelings are harbored and prevents the message from being distorted. Additionally, you might also want to pick a time when everyone is neutral to convey your boundary. This will avoid any unprecedented arguments.

With the knowledge you have garnered in this chapter, you are set to start making better decisions to protect your mental and emotional health. Remember that taking care of yourself and setting boundaries is not a crime. Rather, it is a necessity and one of the best gifts you can give yourself in this stressful time we live in.

However, with all that said, it is also in your best interests to solicit a strong support system. Because no matter how tough you can be, we all need people we can fall back on in dire times.

# 7

# TIP #5: BUILDING A SUPPORT SYSTEM

As human beings, we all have the innate desire to belong and to be understood. And, while other people prefer to be alone, no one can truly live and thrive in isolation.

In the world we live in, where technological advances are taking over as a form of communication, it is so easy for one to overlook the importance of actual human company. Having people that you can trust and rely on for support is an incredible tool for overcoming the stress of modernity.

This is because most people's stress stems from feelings of loneliness and exclusion. However, with the various ways there are to fill this void, that shouldn't be a way of life.

This chapter is centered around helping you develop a strong, stable, and reliable support system. This can include friends, family, and even social workers and therapists.

Essentially, by the end of this chapter, you will learn how to get out there, meet new people, and build long-lasting connections as a way of managing your stress.

## BENEFITS OF A SUPPORT SYSTEM

Many studies have advocated the psychological benefits of social connectedness (Cherry, 2023). It has been found that it reduces symptoms of stress and related disorders such as Post Traumatic Stress Disorder (PTSD), anxiety, and depression. But that's not all. A stable support system can even increase your years on Earth!

Individuals who spend sufficient amounts of time engaging in social activities and in other meaningful social interactions are less likely to suffer from stress. The following two scenarios vividly demonstrate the discrepancy between those who are with and without support systems.

## Scenario 1- Brandon

Adjusting to life after college has been a challenge for 24-year-old Brandon. After moving to an entirely new city and searching for a job, he has never felt lonelier. His college friends have relocated too and are all living completely different lives; some are newlyweds, and others are still finding their balance in the hustle and bustle of urbanization.

To worsen this, his family dynamics aren't the most favorable either. He doesn't get along with his siblings, and his sickly mother is always in and out of the hospital. For this reason, he hardly communicated with anyone, and this hasn't been too kind to his mental health.

As a young engineer who is still trying to establish himself in a professional setting, things don't always go his way. Brandon faces countless challenges adapting to the demands of his work while also trying to grow his career, and after a long, stressful day at work, he has no one he can vent to.

Not having anyone to share his problems with makes him sad, alone, and at times, feel worthless, further increasing his stress levels.

But this is the complete opposite for Tanya.

**Scenario 2- Tanya**

Twenty-two-year-old Tanya is a mom and a bank teller by profession, with a long list of job demands and a busy personal life. She often has a lot of information and customer inquiries to administer to the point that her work gets unbearable. In other words, her fast-paced environment forces her to work harder than usual each day.

To top this is the lack of job security in her company. People are constantly getting retrenched and fired right in front of her eyes, and this is something she finds to be unsettling.

However, despite the stressful nature of her job, she has a supportive community of friends and family she can always look to. Tanya doesn't have to bottle up her emotions for too long, as she always has someone she can talk to. This has been extremely beneficial for managing her stress levels.

### *How Does Having a Solid Social Network Prevent Stress*

Imagine your car suddenly breaking down, and you are all alone, versus your car breaking down while you are with a trusted friend. Or, perhaps going through a break-up without a shoulder to cry on versus having someone by your side? It is a no-brainer that having someone to comfort us in the face of difficulty can be uplifting.

As we discussed earlier in the book, when our bodies sense a perceived threat, they react by releasing stress hormones cortisol and adrenaline. These hormones are crucially helpful in dealing with momentary stressors. However, in the case of chronic stress, these hormones cause multiple mental and physical damage to the body. With the stressful nature of daily life, one can certainly find themselves at the risk of suffering these consequences.

On the contrary, spending time with positive-minded company can counteract this. The good vibes and feelings that you get from positive social interactions allow your body to release "happy" hormones, which neutralize the effects of stress hormones (Reid, 2023).

For this reason, finding a group of people who have your back can really work wonders for your stress levels. In addition to that, it can boost your overall health by promoting self-care, healthier habits, and cognitive functioning.

This is not to imply that the sole purpose of socialization is to have a company around you. The kind of people you associate with truly matters in how well you manage your stress. It is always crucial to stay as far away as possible from toxic people.

### *How to Spot Toxic People*

A Negative or toxic company not only causes stress but also exacerbates existing stress levels. This is because negative social encounters also spur the release of stress hormones.

No matter what, you will come across people who don't serve you at some point in your life. This is a normal part of life that we cannot avoid. But, what we can do is readily equip ourselves with knowledge on diverting and protecting ourselves from toxicity. This will help you avoid the addition of unnecessary stress and instead allow you to focus your efforts on more fruitful things. Here are some great ways to spot toxic people from miles away.

### They Are Attention-Seeking

Watch out for people who are overly dependent on you. Unrelenting phone calls, text messages, attempts to see you, and even randomly showing up at your workplace are all signs. You may also notice that they are always in need of emotional support, while they hardly reciprocate it.

## Unpredictable Behaviors

Are they always hot and cold? On and off? Or maybe they are totally fond of you one minute, and then in the next, they want nothing to do with you. This unpredictable and inconsistent behavior is brutal to adjust to and bad for your mental health.

## Your Relationship with Them Is Always Dramatic

Does drama seem to be dogging their every step? If so, it is a big red flag, and certainly not by chance. One thing that characterizes toxic people is their everlasting quest to provoke others and cause fights. Primarily, this is because they don't have the desire to live harmoniously with other people.

## They Are Manipulative

Toxic people will go to extra lengths to get people to do whatever they want. They lie, hide things from you, and make you feel like you are the reason for their behavior. One way or another, your sixth sense will tell you that you are being taken advantage of.

## They Abuse Drugs or Alcohol

Another huge red flag of toxicity is substance abuse. People who depend on substances to give them character usually inflict physical and emotional harm on those around them.

Toxic People don't typically display their toxicity from the get-go. They lure you with kind gestures, gifts, and other nice incentives, only to unveil their true selves later on.

The relationships in our lives are synonymous with gardens. If you water a rose bush, it will bloom, brighten your garden, and spread beautiful aromas to the vicinity. Conversely, watering a bunch of weeds will only cause them to take over the garden and suck out any beauty it possesses. Positive people are an excellent addition to your life who will make it a lot easier, while toxic people make your life much harder than it ought to be. This is why it is important to 'water' selectively and remove any weeds from your 'garden'.

### Handling Toxic People

Toxic People can be friends, colleagues, or even family members. However, since you now know what toxicity looks and feels like, you can take the necessary steps to boot it out of your life. The following are some tips on protecting yourself from people who don't serve you.

- Confront them regarding their behavior. This will let them know that you are onto them, and if they realize it's wrong, they will apologize.

- Tighten your bolts around them to ensure that their uncomfortable behavior doesn't affect you.
- Remove them from your life if their behavior persists despite your attempts to let them know how it makes you feel.

Based on everything we've discussed in this chapter, it is evident that a social network can help to reduce stress. But did you know that social connectivity can also make you more resilient?

### How Does Social Support Foster Resilience?

Resilience is a crucial attribute to have when it comes to dealing with stress. It keeps you mentally prepared to face challenges and, moreover, to overcome them.

The link between social support and resilience is highly remarkable but very rarely noticed. There are many ways that positive interactions can make you more hardy and able to adapt during challenging times. Here are some of them:

- **Emotional Buffering:** Trusted friends and family provide comfort and understanding during challenges, reducing the impact of stressors.

- **Perspective Shift:** Social connections offer diverse viewpoints and insights, helping reframe situations more positively.
- **Problem-Solving:** Supportive networks offer practical advice and assistance, aiding in finding solutions to problems.
- **Validation:** Feeling understood and validated by others enhances self-esteem and coping abilities. Furthermore, having people who love and understand you reduces sentiments of loneliness and strengthens emotional well-being.

### *Nurturing Healthy Relationships*

A while ago, I was the girl who always preferred to keep to herself, but little did I know this was doing me more harm than good. A feeling of overwhelm and despair characterized my narrative, and this was because I chose to bottle my emotions up. As a result of not having a support structure, my stress mounted and became unbearable.

However, it wasn't until I had episodes of headaches that landed me in the doctor's office that things changed for me. The doctor told me that my persistent headaches were the result of stress and then proceeded to give me advice on how I could reduce it.

Among the list of suggestions made was me getting more social time, and I decided to follow through with it. Since I had always been an avid reader, the first thing that came to my mind was joining the local book club. This soon proved to be one of the best decisions I have ever made.

Rubbing shoulders with like-minded people made it easier for me to create strong and long-lasting friendships. For the first time in a long time, I felt I belonged and accommodated. The burden of my many stressors started to get lighter day by day. Having people that I could resonate with and share my problems with made my life a lot easier, and I've never looked back. I now actively seek to expand my circle of positivity with every opportunity life hands me. And, if I could do it, you can too!

Your support system is just a few steps away. All you need to know is how to rewire yourself to get out of your head and out there, and the rest is history. Let us go through some effective tips for building solid relationships.

- **Be Genuine:** Be authentic and true to yourself in your interactions.
- **Active Listening:** Listen attentively to your friends, showing empathy and understanding.

- **Initiate Communication:** Reach out regularly to maintain a connection.
- **Celebrate Success:** Rejoice in each other's achievements and milestones.
- **Forgiveness:** Be willing to forgive and move past misunderstandings.
- **Honesty:** Communicate your feelings and concerns honestly and respectfully.

A support system doesn't only consist of family and friends. Therapists and psychologists are also available to give you a shoulder to cry on and advice during trying times.

### *Resources and Professionals Available for Support*

Due to several factors, such as the environment and availability of relatable personalities, forming new relationships can be hard. However, this is not to say there's nothing else that can be done. When you sense that there is no one you can trust or relate to, you can always talk to a mental health specialist. Therapists and psychologists are well-versed in the works of the mind and can help you navigate stressful situations. There are numerous therapies you can attend to manage your stress levels. The following are some of them:

**Cognitive Behavioral Therapy (CBT)**

This is the most approached form of therapy. In CBT, you work with the therapist to analyze your behaviors and thought patterns to identify your possible stressors (Cherney, 2020). Once this is done, you will find sustainable stress-coping strategies. CBT can be both long-term and short-term, depending on the severity of your stress. Chronic stress will need long-term sessions, while acute stress may require short-term sessions. With this method of therapy, you can also expect help with stress-related disorders such as anxiety, depression, and insomnia.

**Behavioral Therapy**

The idea behind this type of therapy is similar to that of CBT in the sense that it focuses on behavioral deviations over time. However, the difference is that it does not focus on the cognitive part of things. Behavioral therapy helps you to make alterations to your current actions to prepare you to deal with stress even in the future. So, it is more of a long-term solution to stress.

**Group Therapy**

This kind of therapy is particularly crucial for those struggling to come to terms with traumatic experiences (Cherney, 2020). Such experiences can be sexual assault, natural disasters, divorce, or the loss of a loved one. A typical group therapy session would have a group of patients, each with their unique experience, being guided by a therapist. Patients usually use the sharing of their experiences as a means to bring a sense of togetherness and sympathy.

You can now translate the knowledge you have learned about building a strong support system into your life. It may take some trial and error until you find the right group of people, but what is needed is patience and consistency.

Another issue that affects our stress levels is time management and productivity. These are crucial components of our everyday lives that we must manage well. To learn more about how you can do this, let us go into the next chapter, where we will discuss it in more depth.

# 8

# TIP #6: TIME MANAGEMENT AND PRODUCTIVITY

Time is an asset that must be used wisely to ensure that maximum productivity is yielded. But, in this seemingly organized human culture, it is actually surprising to know that not many of us are organized when it comes to time management. In fact, a survey conducted on a group of working-class individuals backed this up (Richardson, 2022). Out of 500 people, only 18% had a proper time management schedule. The rest just haphazardly took on tasks as they emerged in the hopes that they would get everything done at once (Richardson, 2022).

The issue of time management is the reason many of us still find ourselves pinned down by stress. It makes us feel out of control and like our days are extremely short.

What if I told you that you don't have to go to bed feeling unaccomplished any longer? We will be addressing all the issues related to time management in this chapter. You will learn how to be time-savvy and how to get your to-do list fitted into the 24-hour day while still leaving yourself with leisure time. So, delve right in and find out how you can capitalize your time and make the most of your day.

## TIME AS A STRESS FACTOR

Time is seemingly abundant when we are in school. We feel like the day is taking forever to come to an end, and we just can't wait for the weekend to come. However, the opposite is true in adulthood. With all the tasks and obligations that weigh us down, 24 hours seems never enough. We panic while doing everything because we are out of time. From the very start of the day, you may find yourself showering, getting dressed, and leaving the house in a rush. Sometimes, because time isn't on your side, you even skip breakfast.

Constantly feeling like you have a lot to do can trigger your fight or flight mechanism, causing you to become stressed. This has become the narrative of most people in the modern day. One such example is Jayden, who struggles to keep up with time, and it's getting the best of him.

Jayden is a successful blog writer with a booming career, a Mass Communication degree on the way, and a lively social life. A typical day in his life is spent chasing word counts and studying for upcoming tests. Since he is a social butterfly, he also makes time to see his buddies during his already busy schedule.

This is something he can only keep up with at times; however, other times, it gets too much for him to handle. The looming deadlines, assignments, tests, and the demands of his social life constantly haunt him. No matter how much work he tries to get done, he still feels like he's done nothing. This makes him feel stressed and upset, and at times, he even feels useless. For Jayden, the lack of time and his poor time management are the leading cause of his stress. If only he could plan his days better and use his time wisely, his stress levels would be a lot lower than they are.

### Time's Impact on Stress and Burnout

On a scale of 1 to 10, how would you rate your time management? Do you have tasks endlessly piling up that it's making you feel so spent and unable to cope with life in general?

Poor time management can have many detrimental effects on the quality of your health. Let us look at some ways it can bring stress into your life.

- **Procrastination:** Procrastination syndrome can cause the delay of tasks. This, in turn, can lead to last-minute pressure, a hefty workload, and intensifying stress.
- **Overcommitment:** Poor planning can result in taking on more tasks than manageable, causing overwhelm.
- **Missed Deadlines:** Poor time allocation leads to missed deadlines, causing stress and anxiety.
- **Lack of Balance:** Not only is it important to have time for your work obligations, but also for your personal needs. Neglecting personal time strains well-being, heightening stress.
- **Constant Pressure:** Poor time management creates a perpetual sense of urgency, which can worsen stress levels.

Conversely, planning your events and time appropriately can enhance your well-being and make life a lot more enjoyable.

### The Link Between Time Management and Well-Being

Being more time-conscious has been largely associated with a better quality of life. Managing your time accordingly can help you to keep your stress at bay and have a sense of control and direction over your life.

However, that isn't all. Keeping track of your time can also:

- **Enhance Productivity:** Efficiently managed time leads to accomplished tasks and a sense of achievement.
- **Physical Health:** Well-structured days allow time for exercise, contributing to physical well-being.
- **Quality Rest:** Proper time management ensures adequate sleep and relaxation.
- **Work-Life Balance:** Allocating time for work, hobbies, and rest fosters a balanced and fulfilling life.
- **Personal Growth:** Time for learning and personal development enriches well-being.

Now that you know all the ways bad and good time management can affect you, it may be time to learn of some ways to get your time to work for you and not against you.

### Effective Time Management Techniques

Life can get busy to the point where only a fine line separates work and leisure. However, for you to live the best life possible, it is essential to re-establish a clear boundary between the two.

This is where a time management technique comes in. By making use of an effective time management technique, you will be able to budget your time more efficiently. Moreover, you will be empowered to get more done each day. This can bring more success and less stress to your life and, in many instances, give your confidence a boost. A number of time management techniques have been tried, tested, and found to work. Let us take a look at some of them.

**Find Out How You Spend Your Time**

Time is said to be money, so it may be useful to keep count of how you spend your time like you would with your dollars. This means closely analyzing your day-to-day tendencies where time is concerned. How much time do you spend being productive versus being non-productive? If your time expenditure is inclined towards non-productivity, especially when you have a lot to do, it may be time to shift your priorities.

**Avoid Rigid Routines, instead be Flexible but Intentional**

If you are one to say, "I will surely get ABCD done within four hours, etc." you should bear in mind that things don't always work out as planned. Despite our best efforts to get organized, life happens and will always happen. At times, we exaggerate our ability to get things done within a given time frame, only to end up disappointed. This is a phenomenon that is formally recognized as a "planning fallacy." To counteract this, it is important to be flexible yet intentional. This implies planning your day's tasks flexibly but with the intention of focusing on each task to ensure you complete it in a timely manner. Another thing to keep in mind is that your priorities will shift from day to day. Therefore, you should always work in order of your priorities and ensure that you give each task your undivided attention.

## Prioritize

To-do lists are great for time management; however, they can get lengthy to the point that they invoke confusion rather than organization.

The main prerogative behind making a to-do list is not just listing a number of tasks that need to be taken care of. Rather, it is tactfully prioritizing your tasks to ensure that each one is done eventually. Time-management matrices such as the Eisenhower Matrix are great tools to exploit for this. This is because they provide guidance on how you can best categorize your tasks to ensure productivity. This is how they work.

- *Urgent (must be done immediately)*: These tasks have looming deadlines and must be done as a matter of urgency.

- *Schedule for later*: These tasks are crucial but not urgent and can be dealt with later.
- *Delegate:* These tasks are best handled by someone else. Examples are mowing the lawn or fixing the damaged water pipes in the house.
- *Delete*: These tasks are simply "space fillers," add no value to your goal, and therefore can be deleted from your to-do lists.

## Deal With the Most Difficult Thing First

Distractions are inevitable, and in most cases, they get in the way of us achieving the main purpose of our day. Be it taking out the cat litter, doing the dishes, or answering dozens of emails, all these "small" tasks can pile up to consume most of our day, leaving almost no time to complete the more significant and most relevant tasks. This is precisely why Brian Tracy, a leadership expert, came up with the genius idea of "Eat That Frog". Eating that frog means getting the most challenging and most daunting task off your list first thing in the morning. Then, only after accomplishing this task can you proceed to do other obligations. Although this productivity method can benefit everyone, it is specifically recommended for those who usually procrastinate or postpone tasks for later.

## No Matter What You Do, Do Not Multitask

Multitasking thwarts productivity. Taking on too many tasks at once results in merely being "busy" and not actually being "productive." When you stumble from one task to another without actually getting anything done, you are being "busy" as opposed to being productive. This doesn't yield any accomplishment at the end of the day but instead leads to a perpetual cycle of endlessly tackling the same tasks.

## The Pomodoro Technique

This is yet another "golden" time management tool that has proven to work well for those who work with deadlines. It involves breaking down daunting tasks into smaller, more manageable assignments. For instance, if you are working on a writing project, you may estimate that you need four hours to reach your target goals. Space your tasks as follows:

- **First hour (09:00-10:00):** Work for 50 minutes and take a break for 10 minutes.
- **Second hour (10:00-11:00):** work for 50 minutes and take a break for 10 minutes, and so on.

Your only mission during these time blocks is to switch to laser focus mode and divert all distractions. This may mean turning off your pop-up notifications or switching your phone off altogether. By following this technique, you will be sure to meet your targets and still get time to take care of other errands.

Apart from these techniques, there are many other ways to keep track of time. Productivity specialists have devised multiple time-management apps that promote better time efficiency.

*Most Recommended Time-Management Apps*

Manually written to-do lists can easily get lost, forcing us to constantly make new ones. What won't get lost is a time-management app. Modernity has made it possible for us to record our tasks in an easy and accessible manner. With time-management apps, you will be able to use your smartphone as the center of administration for all your tasks. The best part is that there is an app for everyone. Whether you are a teacher wanting to plan lessons ahead of time or a highly obligated business owner, there is an app made with your needs at heart. Behold, productivity is made simpler.

**#1 Rated App for Work Schedules - Toggl**

Due to its ability to work hand in hand with other apps, this tool is a go-to for professionals such as freelancers and entrepreneurs who spend most of their time working digitally.

## #1 Rated App for Personal Matters - TimeTree

TimeTree is specially designed per the needs of families. This app allows the members of a family to store their to-do list, making it easier to get organized as a family.

## #1 Rated App for Delegations - Trello

If you are a project manager whose work revolves around delegating tasks and ensuring that all project operations run smoothly, then this is the app for you. Trello has a feature that allows you to micromanage tasks and make sure that all delegated assignments are completed in a timely manner.

## #1 Rated App for Additional Resources - Calendar

Calendar specializes in analytics, which helps you to adjust your time disposition more appropriately. It has a feature that times all the activities you do to give you a verdict on whether you have had a productive day or not.

## #1 Rated App for Multiple Platforms - Remember the Milk

If you are a jack of all trades, this one's for you. No matter how many tasks and projects you've got going on at once, you can keep everything organized in one place. Remember, the Milk has diversified access, meaning you can use it on several gadgets such as phones, laptops, and even wearables.

With these time management apps, you'll surely be able to make every minute count. Since they all have a free version available, you can access them at zero cost. Not only will you get the "work stuff" done, but you will also find time to unwind and be you.

### Balancing Productivity and Relaxation

Whether you work at the office or at home, you have, at one point in your life, watched your work life seep into your leisure time. It can be extremely frustrating when this happens. Instead of watching that movie that has recently dropped, you have to tackle unfinished work. Or, perhaps, if you had planned to take an early night, you might find yourself answering work-related texts and emails until late. Despite our efforts to keep this from happening, it is bound to happen if we don't take active preventative measures. However, with the following list of tips on separating your work time from relaxation, that should become a thing of the past.

- **Set Boundaries:** Establish clear work hours and stick to them to prevent overworking.
- **Time Blocking:** ensure that you allocate specific time blocks for work tasks and leisure activities. Doing this makes sure that your

schedule is always balanced, thus reducing your risk of burning out.

- **Limit Screen Time:** It may be helpful to set limits on work-related digital activities outside work hours. This is because even after work, our professional responsibilities continue to haunt us through our gadgets. Be certain that you disconnect from work emails and notifications during your leisure time.

- **Take Breaks:** Brief breaks are essential during working hours. They give you time to recharge and gain perspective amid a hectic assignment.

- **Avoid Overcommitment:** Remember that everything in life works best when there is a balance to it. Say no to additional work if it affects your leisure time.

- **Family and Friends Time:** Dedicate quality time to loved ones to free your mind and restore balance.

### Why Relaxation Matters

All too often, we hear phrases like "sleep is for the dead" and "if you aren't always busy, you are lazy." Such perceptions of relaxation are extraordinarily harmful and perpetuate the idea that working relentlessly and not resting are virtues that determine your success. As you may be familiar with the saying, "All work and no play makes Jack a dull boy," how well you rest is a more relevant way of measuring your success.

One thing is for sure: most successful people know how to sit back and relax. This is because being successful requires that you take great care of your well-being.

Take time to escape the rat race and think back to the activity you absolutely love but don't have time for anymore. It could be as simple as having dinner dates with your best friend or even star gazing in the navy-blue night sky. It could be anything!

Whatever it is, make sure to incorporate it back into your life. Leisure activities are equally important as the other components of your to-do list. Just as you would make sure to check the financial report or take your car in for repairs, your relaxation time should be mandatory. In fact, it should be a set part of your schedule that stays put regardless of what comes up.

Prioritizing relaxation is not only great for establishing a work-life balance but also enhances your overall state of health. It has been found to improve heart health, cognitive, and immune functioning. Hopefully, this will come to mind any time you think of skipping your leisure time to take care of work matters.

From everything you have read in this chapter, I hope you clearly understand just how big a role time management plays in your life. It is equally a deal breaker as it is a deal maker. This is why it is crucial to learn to use your time wisely and ensure that you remain productive in all that you do.

We have, however, come this far into the book without having a detailed discussion on how physical activity can be a powerful tool in stress reduction. This is our topic in the next chapter. Let us move into chapter 9, where you will learn how to use physical activity as a way to catapult yourself to wellness.

# 9

# TIP #7: PHYSICAL HEALTH AND STRESS REDUCTION

Stress has become an omnipresent aspect of modern life. Whether you are a clerk, a doctor, or a homemaker, stress doesn't discriminate. We are all bound to face it at one point or another in our lives. However, in the midst of all the turmoil and mental emancipation lies a potent remedy that has been endlessly applauded for its effectiveness in stress reduction—physical activity.

Staying active is not only a key weapon in reducing stress but also vital for preventing it and encouraging better overall health. This leads us to the seventh official tip of this book.

In this chapter, we will be exploring the intricate relationship between physical activity and stress levels.

With the valuable guidelines and tips at your disposal, you will learn how to incorporate fitness and a nutritious diet into your daily routine to create the life you've always wanted. Without waiting any longer, let us begin to unpack all you need to know about the link between physical and stress reduction.

## THE LINK BETWEEN EXERCISE AND STRESS

The common notion is that only rest can relieve stress, but did you know that exercise can do that much better? This is because making time to be active results in the release of endorphins (Harvard Health Publishing, 2020).

These are also called "happy hormones" and do a fantastic job at counteracting the stress hormones cortisol and adrenaline, which plague our bodies during stressful times. Essentially, exercise can be viewed as the calm of the storm, and this has been well acknowledged over the course of humanity. Alexander Pope once said, "The strength of the mind is not rest but exercise. (Harvard Health Publishing, 2020)."

How much can physical activity really alleviate stress? You may wonder. The following narrative on my personal experience with physical activity answers that question and more.

Being as busy as I was and having a lot on my plate, staying active was always something that I dreaded. I felt like it took great effort and was very time-consuming.

To be honest, I only felt like having the added obligation of exercising would only add to my gigantic pile of work. So, I kept going on, marching like a soldier because I thought I could do without it, but my stress only became worse.

Mentally, I felt exhausted and like I was out of this world. I couldn't bring myself to focus on anything, as my brain was fogged. Physically, I suffered muscle aches, headaches, chest pains, and an overwhelming sense of fatigue.

This was until my doctor recommended that I exercise at least every other day. With that, I got rid of my previous perceptions of exercise and decided to venture into it for my own good. Staying active helped me feel well again. For the first time in a long time, I did not feel like my life was coming down crashing; it was like it was a wholly new me. My mood was instantly boosted, I became more resilient, and my life was a lot more manageable. That decision is one that I regret not making earlier on in my life.

We briefly mentioned the link between exercise and the reduction of stress hormones above. Let us delve deeper into it.

**Research on Exercise and Stress Hormones**

Physical exercise provides an influx of neurological chemicals, alternatively known as endorphins, which can instantly improve moods and get rid of stress. Here is how they function in your system:

- **Cortisol Regulation:** Regular exercise helps regulate cortisol levels, preventing the excessive activation of the fight or flight stress response mechanism.
- **Sleep Improvement:** By keeping you restless and making it hard for you to fall asleep, stress can decrease your quality of sleep. Physical activity can contend with this and help restore your normal, healthier sleeping habits.
- **Improved Mind-Body Connection:** Exercise serves as a distraction from stressors by engaging the mind and increasing the connection and correspondence between the body and the mind.

Stress levels differ across people. No one's stress is the same as the other; however, no matter how acute or chronic your stress may be, there is a solution for everyone.

## *Exercise for Different Stress Levels*

Exercise is dynamic, and since different things appeal to different people, it is important to find what ticks your boxes. All kinds of exercises do a phenomenal job of keeping stress levels relatively low. But what you should know is that engaging in an exercise you truly enjoy is what takes the game up a notch. For this reason, it is of utmost importance to find something you will absolutely love to do.

By doing this, exercise won't feel like a chore but rather an escape point and a place of peace amidst trying times. Furthermore, finding the exercise enjoyable will only create consistency and dedication to it in the long run. The following lists should help you decide on the type of exercise that best suits you and your stress level.

## Low-Stress Levels

- *Gentle yoga or stretching:* Yoga and stretching are simple yet effective ways of relinquishing stress. These exercises are slow, controlled movements and poses balanced with mindful deep breathing to improve the mind-body connection. Yoga relaxes your body and mind by activating your body's natural calming mechanism. However, if you are new to it, you may want to go for simpler alternatives such as "gentle yoga" or yoga for beginners. Other forms of yoga, such as "power yoga," may not be the most ideal for combating stress as they are too rigorous.

- *Tai Chi*: The idea behind tai chi is very similar to that of yoga in the sense that both exercises include self-paced mindful movements. Even though Tai Chi is a derivative of martial arts, it has calming properties that can restore your balance and help you deal with stress. Apart from that, tai chi also offers a long list of benefits—making it an indispensable part of fitness. Studies have found that it can boost bone health, improve immune function, and help shield its participants from heart-related illnesses and fibromyalgia. It is also very convenient. You can take advantage of any moment and any place to practice it, making it easier for you to gel it into your daily routine.

## Moderate Stress

- *Brisk walking or jogging*: Brisk walking and jogging increase your breathing and heart rate.

This allows oxygen to be transported to the brain at a faster rate, encouraging the release of mood-boosting hormones and chemicals. Moreover, it is mindfulness in motion. It allows you to be mindful as you move, therefore fortifying the mind-body connection even further.

- *Hiking:* This activity is a wonderful balance of exercise and quality time with nature. Just like moving your body releases stress, scenic views also promote the production and release of mood-boosting chemicals.

## High Stress

- *High-intensity interval training (HIIT):* Although HIIT can work for people at all different stress levels, it is particularly praised for its stress reduction among those who struggle with insurmountable stress. But that isn't all; a study conducted by the University of Arizona divulged that HIIT can increase job satisfaction by up to 19% (8 Exercises That Relieve Stress— Women's Guide to Stress Management - Everyday Health, 2011). The more satisfied you are about your job, the less likely it is to stress you. Moreover, because workouts usually span over a few minutes, it will not dent your schedule in any way.

- *Kickboxing*: This form of exercise revolves around carefully orchestrated kicking and punching, usually without the intent to cause harm. It has been found that high-intensity exercises do an exceptional job of mitigating extremely high-stress levels (8 Exercises That Relieve Stress - Women's Guide to Stress Management - Everyday Health, 2011). Since kickboxing is high-intensity, it is an excellent choice. It serves as a healthy outlet for negative emotions that stem from stressful situations.

A crucial and often overlooked factor in stress relief is nutrition. Eating healthy not only protects you from various physical ailments but is also an effective way to combat the stress of day-to-day life.

## NUTRITION AND STRESS MANAGEMENT

While acute stress can suppress all cravings and appetite, the opposite can be said for chronic stress. As your body constantly "fights off" perceived threats, it demands a surplus of calories. Often, this leads to cravings for unhealthy foods such as sugary drinks, and overly processed, and fatty foods.

Although it may feel satisfying to eat all these comfort foods, our health suffers eventually. This may aggravate the already dangerous effects of stress on our health, leaving it in a ditch. For this reason, it is absolutely important to watch what we put in our mouths. Eating healthy can counter the determinants of stress and lower its risk of occurring. Let us read through Kaitlyn's narrative to get a more profound understanding of the role healthy eating plays on stress levels.

Having suffered from stress for a long time, Kaitlyn had always been one to give in to her unhealthy cravings. They seemed to keep her going when she needed a "pick me up," and she became heavily reliant on her sugar and fat-filled diet to get her through her emotional and mental decline.

However, when the time came for her regular check-ups, the scale had unwelcome surprises for her. Kaitlyn, who previously had a slim frame, kept putting on pounds. It was clear that her eating habits were getting the best of her and not actually helping her alleviate her stress.

Concerned about the way in which her image had been distorted, she took to the internet to look for various healthy diets she could eat to improve both her physical and mental health. With the information she found, she formed a weekly eating plan.

She purged her kitchen of all food that wasn't nourishing and instead replaced it with nourishing and wholesome items. In just a week of adhering to this new lifestyle, she could already feel the difference. Kaitlyn had a boost in energy and could focus for longer. Emotionally, she felt great, too! Her stress was down, and her mood was a lot better than it had been before. Kaitlyn was relishing in the benefits of her newfound nutrient-rich diet.

As it is evident from Kaitlyn's story, nutritious eating is imperative for living a life of very little stress. The advantages of eating well are broad. Here are some of a good diet's biggest influences on your health.

- **Regulation of hormones:** Eating a nutritious and well-balanced diet can aid the stabilization of stress hormones such as cortisol and adrenaline.
- **Energy Levels:** Stress can lead to fatigue. Consuming healthy meals can help to boost your energy levels and reverse the exhausting effects of stress.
- **Brain Function:** When it comes to dealing with stress, efficient cognitive functioning is of extreme importance. This is something that a nutrient-rich diet can help you to achieve.

By now, you surely know that if you are to overcome your stress, the bags of Doritos and the Coke cans won't do you justice. What you may not know is how exactly you should begin restructuring your diet and what foods you should eat. The answer is only a few words away.

### Stress Reducing Foods and Supplements

In a world full of quick-fix foods such as takeout and unhealthy packaged foods also lies a haven of nutrient-dense foods. Below are some foods you can count on in the midst of challenging times.

### Oatmeal

Oats are a source of complex carbohydrates, which also contain mood-boosting agents. Having a serving of oatmeal here and there can help stabilize your blood sugar levels and hamper the release of stress hormones (Doran, 2021). By encouraging the release of stress hormones such as serotonin, it aids relaxation and stress reduction. To optimize these benefits, avoid adding refined sugar to your oatmeal. You can add pieces of fresh or dried fruits to add a layer of natural sweetness.

**Salmon and Tuna**

These omega-3-rich foods play an instrumental role in stabilizing stress hormones. Besides that, they have been proven to effectively reverse stress-related illnesses such as stroke, high blood pressure, depression, and heart failure (Doran, 2021). If you don't eat fish, don't worry. Vegan alternatives such as spinach, flaxseed, and walnuts also provide a valuable quantity of Omega-3 fatty acids.

**Dark Chocolate**

If you have a sweet tooth, you don't have to worry about feeling guilty after eating dark chocolate. It keeps cortisol controlled in the body while also providing several antioxidants that fight the symptoms of heart disease. While it is definitely a healthy treat, be on the lookout for dark chocolate desserts, as they may have slightly more sugar. The best kind of dark chocolate would be the one which is made up of predominantly 70% cocoa.

**Chamomile tea**

Chamomile tea has long been praised for its stress-relief properties. Due to the sedative and muscle-calming substances, it is great for soothing upset stomachs and headaches associated with stress (Doran, 2021). In addition to that, it can also boost your quality of sleep by far. It is best consumed at the day's end, just before going to bed.

By incorporating these foods into your diet, you will feel a lot better in your skin. All you have to do is to be determined and consistent with healthy eating.

Stress can sometimes distort sleeping patterns. Read on to find out how you can start getting the quality sleep you deserve after a long day at work.

### Stress and Its Impact on Sleep

If you struggle to fall asleep on most nights, stress might be standing in the way of you and a good night's sleep. When you are stressed, endless thoughts about work, school, finances, and other personal matters take over your mind and keep you from sleeping.

This is because stress extends the amount of time that it takes for you to doze off and cuts your sleep into fragments (CDC, 2022). Nonetheless, there are many ways to change your narrative and help you count sheep better at night. Below are some of them.

- **Consistent Schedule:** Maintain regular sleep and wake times, even on weekends.
- **Create a Restful Environment:** Make your sleep space comfortable, dark, and quiet.

- **Limit Screen Time:** Avoid screens (phones, computers, TVs) before bedtime.
- **Relaxation Routine:** Engage in calming activities like reading, meditation, or gentle stretches before bed.
- **Limit Stimulants:** Avoid caffeine and heavy meals close to bedtime.
- **Physical Activity:** Regular exercise supports better sleep but avoid intense workouts close to bedtime.

These tips should help you get more rest and wake up rejuvenated.

Hopefully, from everything you have learned in this chapter, you will be better able to take care of your physical health as a means of dealing with stress. Keeping active and eating healthy will be important factors in your journey to recovery. For that reason, you should remember to incorporate it into your day-to-day life.

Now that we have discussed everything on the importance of taking good care of your physical health, it is time to move into the next chapter. Here, we will be talking about the ways you can embrace change and find fulfillment in your quest to discover your stress-free self.

# 10

## TIP #8: EMBRACING CHANGE AND FINDING FULFILLMENT

If you take time to look into the bounds of nature, you will see that rivers change course in adaptation to the ever-changing terrain. Above the Earth, stars change position as the days go by, signifying the unmatched power in embracing the flow and ebb of life. Just like the various elements and components of nature were made with the innate ability to adapt to ever-changing circumstances, so were we. Any human, from all walks of Earth, is capable of adapting to new circumstances and ways of life.

This is the sentiment behind the eighth and last tip of this book. In this chapter, we will focus on all the ways you can prepare yourself to dance to life's unpredictable tunes. By the end of this chapter, you will understand what it truly means to bend but not break.

Moreover, you will not only learn to stand tall during challenges but also to sway confidently with each twist and turn in your narrative.

## THE NATURE OF CHANGE

Think back to the past six years of your life. Is it still the way it was back then, or has it changed? Maybe you have restructured your friendship groups, adopted a new style of dressing, or perhaps even got your first car?

This goes to show how life never stays the same. Change is life, and life is change, and the act of accepting change can be seen as a way of solidifying our existence on Earth. By embracing change, you show that you are one with life and that you are willing to learn and grow from all of life's experiences. Many individuals are letting change into their lives and aren't afraid to go through it. One such example is Brian, who is taking every day as it comes.

Brian had worked numerous jobs throughout his life. From teaching to freelancing and back to teaching again, one can rightfully say he's seen it all. Apart from his stints in different jobs, he decided to kick a long-time drinking habit for good and began a journey of sobriety. This wasn't easy to do, but it was a necessary part of his life he had to accept.

Not so long after that, he and the love of his life joined in holy matrimony, which meant that his family had doubled. The married life took some time to adjust to, but like always, he remained adaptive. And, as we all know, some people only come into our lives temporarily; Brian had to let go of some friends, too.

For his benefit, he cut off all friendships that did not define nor serve him anymore, deciding to rediscover his passing for writing. With that, he has since become a well-established publisher who has a wide variety of books on the philosophy of life.

Brian understands fully that today will never be the same as tomorrow; therefore, he keeps his heart and mind open to whatever course his life takes.

**Moment of thought:** Take the idea behind Brian's story and place it in the context of your life. Think of all the things that have changed over the past few years (good and bad). Though you might not have known it, you have been strong—that's the only reason you are here and still going strong. That alone should be a testament that no matter how much life deviates, you can make it through even the most turbulent circumstances. All you need to do is to keep embracing change wholeheartedly.

However, it must be brought to light that embracing change comes with its challenges. This is where goal-setting steps in. Setting goals can help us navigate life in the face of adversity, keeping us in the direction of our ultimate vision or purpose.

## STRATEGIES FOR SETTING FULFILLING AND REALISTIC GOALS

Goals are an important part of our existence as human beings. They help us realize our dreams and become what we want to become. Nonetheless, determination and willpower aren't the only things that come into play as far as goal setting is concerned. To truly make your dreams a reality, you will need to adopt a goal-setting strategy. The following are some highly recommended strategies for setting goals effectively.

### *HARD Goals*

Each letter in HARD represents; heartfelt, animated, required, and difficult.

- **Heartfelt:** Let's say you want to buy a new home; imagine the joy you would feel one day after having accomplished this goal. Associate this feeling with the goal anytime you think of it. This will serve as your drive to accomplish it.

- **Animated:** Picture yourself, one day, having achieved your goals. Engage your senses to try to imagine what that victory would sound, look, taste, smell, and feel like. You'll surely love it! Each time you think of that goal, let all your sensory attachments to it awaken and fill you up with determination.

- **Required:** It is crucial to keep participating in activities that will keep your determination going. Let's say you would like to become a fashion designer; you can attend fashion shows to keep growing your interest towards your goal.

- **Difficult:** Be sure to set goals that you will find challenging. This will guarantee you a sense of accomplishment at the end of it all.

### One-Word Goals

This strategy revolves around keeping it simple and to the point. All you have to do is link your goal to a single word describing it and use it to propel yourself towards it. This technique is particularly useful for those who are new to the concept of goal setting. For instance, if your goal is to lose 30 pounds (13.61 kg) by the end of the winter, you can link your goal to the word 'run.'

Every time you think of your goal, you will be reminded to 'run' in order to lose weight and accomplish it.

## SMART Goals

Each letter in SMART represents specific, measurable, achievable, realistic, and time-bound.

- **Specific:** Give a concise and clear statement of what your goal is. If your goal is to get a job in the healthcare industry, be particular about the type of job.
- **Measurable:** Give your goal a measurable aspect. For example, if you want to get a position in healthcare, then how many resumes do you intend to submit each week?
- **Achievable:** Can your current schedule accommodate this goal? You have to make sure that you'll actually have enough time to work towards it.
- **Realistic:** Is this something you can actually accomplish at this point in your life? Make sure to aspire realistically.
- **Time-bound:** Set a period for which you aim to have accomplished the goal. This will give you time to actually plan every step towards it.

SMART goals can be further stretched to form SMARTER goals. The added letters in this acronym stand for evaluate and readjust. This is what makes SMARTER goals slightly different from SMART goals:

- **Evaluate:** Take time to evaluate your goals every so often. This will give you an indication of whether you are on track or not.
- **Readjust:** Remember that there will be curveballs. You may get busier than you might anticipate but remember to be flexible and stay on track.

On the notion of goals, it is important to keep the goals from all aspects of your life aligned.

## HOW TO ALIGN PERSONAL GOALS WITH PROFESSIONAL ASPIRATIONS

Since life is all about reaching a point of balance and equilibrium, it is vital to align the goals we set in our personal lives with those in our professional scene. The following are some tips you can use to do this.

- **Clarity:** Define clear personal and professional goals.

- **Prioritization:** Determine what matters most to you in both realms.
- **Balance:** Strive for a balance that allows progress in both personal and professional areas.
- **Time Management:** Allocate time to work on both personal and professional goals.
- **Set Milestones:** Break down goals into achievable milestones for both spheres.
- **Continuous Review:** Regularly assess progress and adjust as needed.

To reach our goals and bring our aspirations to reality, it is indispensable that we learn to let go and move on from certain things, as they may hold us back from progress.

## THE ART OF LETTING GO OF STRESS

While the urge may arise to fight stressors to their very end, there will come a time when letting go becomes the only option. In life, there are things that are beyond our control.

The more we try to fight and change these things, the less time we actually have left to spend on things we can change. When stressing and fighting for a cause is unlikely to change its outcome, it is okay to let go. This calls on us to release all imperfections and understand that life is not meant to be without setbacks. The instant we get to fully acknowledge this marks the very beginning of greater things to come.

I trust that this chapter has reframed your perceptions of life and its ever-changing nature. Personally, I like to look at life as a book that has been written before our existence—what is meant to happen will and what isn't won't, despite our hardest efforts. This understanding is something that has helped me tremendously to make peace with everything that I cannot change.

Hopefully, with the goal-setting techniques we discussed, you will be able to set goals to help you manage your life better and live a more stress-free life.

The end of this chapter marks the last of your suffering in the hands of stress and the beginning of a new life. Stay with me as we go into the next chapter, where your 14-day challenge awaits!

# 11

# 14 DAYS TO A NEW YOU

> *One can choose to go back toward safety or forward toward growth. Growth must be chosen again and again; fear must be overcome again and again.*
>
> — ABRAHAM MASLOW

You have learned all you need to about stress and how you can overcome it. Now, it is time to put that knowledge into action. The time has come to reclaim your life from stress and drive it in the right direction.

This chapter is centered around a structured 14-day challenge to help you discover a new you. Each day will focus on an entirely different aspect of the book to ensure that you are ready to take on the world as a new, stress-free you. Let us wait no more!

## DAY 1: THE JOURNEY BEGINS WITHIN

Today is all about self-introspection, recognizing your stressors, and setting the stage for the next two weeks.

### *A Deep Dive into Introspection*

To truly address the stress in your life, you need to get in touch with your inner self.

- Pick out a quiet moment in your day when you can sit comfortably and in peace. With your eyes closed, take three deep breaths.
- Ask yourself the following questions:
- When was the last time I truly felt relaxed.
- How do my body and mind feel when I'm under stress?
- What causes these feelings to arise the most?

### *Identify Your Stressors*

Now, it's time to get to the bottom of what it is that brings stress into your life.

- Grab a notebook and a pencil or pen.

- Using a ruler to guide you, or with a free hand, draw a straight line down the middle of the page to separate it into two columns.
- In the column on your left-hand side, list all the regularly occurring tasks or situations that make you feel overwhelmed or anxious.
- In the column on the right-hand side, list down all the emotions, feelings, or sensations that usually accompany each situation or task.

Example:

| Situation or Task | Accompanying feelings, emotions, and sensations |
| --- | --- |
| Project deadline at work | Tight chest and racing thoughts |

Recognising these patterns is the first step to addressing your stressors more efficiently.

### Set Achievable Goals

Reflect on the following:

- What would I want to have achieved by the end of this 14-day challenge?
- List two to three realistic goals for the next two weeks. Make sure that these goals are

attainable.

Example:

| |
|---|
| I want to practice deep breathing for five minutes each day. |
| I want to challenge at least one negative thought each day. |
| By the end of these two weeks, I would like to have at least five relaxation activities I can look at. |

**Wrap-up:** Committing to this challenge is a huge step. Keep in mind that the journey to a stress-free you is not a sprint but a marathon, so patience is key in all that you do. Till we meet again tomorrow for day 2!

## DAY 2: HARNESSING THE BENEFITS OF MINDFUL BREATHING

Welcome back! Today's challenge is all about immersing yourself in the soothing realm of mindful breathing. Not only that, but you will also learn how you can incorporate it into your day-to-day life.

### *The Power of Mindful Breathing*

This ancient relaxation technique has been lauded time and time again for its stress-relieving effects. If it has been a go-to stress remedy for countless people all over the globe, then you, too, can reap the benefits.

### *A Moment in Guided Breathing*

1. Look for a calm and quiet place to do this.
2. Sit comfortably, either sitting or lying down.
3. With your eyes shut, take note of your natural breathing pattern, but do not attempt to alter it.
4. Take a deep breath for a count of four as you feel it rejuvenate every single cell in your body.
5. Hold your breath for another count of four.
6. Now, for a count of six, exhale slowly as you imagine all the stress and tension escaping your body.
7. Repeat this for between 5 and 10 minutes, making sure your mind doesn't wander from the present moment.

### *Blending Mindful Breathing into Your Daily Life*

- **Morning awakening:** A five-minute practice as a "coffee" for your soul.
- **Midday recharge:** Take a brief two minutes from your busy afternoon to recollect yourself.
- **Nightly wind-down:** Before you drift away into sleep, let a 10-minute mindful breathing practice be your lullaby.

### *Reflection Time*

Journal your experiences for the day. How did mindful breathing help you during stressful situations? Did you find yourself calmer than you otherwise might have been? Record all your responses in your journal for reference.

Well done for getting through the day mindfully. Here's to breathing your way to a more serene life; cheers!

## DAY 3: CULTIVATING GRATITUDE FOR RESILIENCE

Today is all about uncovering the intricate link between gratitude and resilience. Let us see what's in store for us.

### The Power of Gratitude

Being grateful isn't only great for adding positivity to your life but also for boosting your resilience against stress.

### Gratitude Exercise

With your eyes closed, think of all that you are grateful for today, big or small. As you do this, allow yourself to feel the positive energy each thought brings.

## Gratitude Journaling

Start a dedicated gratitude journal. Every night before you go to sleep, write down everything that made you smile and that you are thankful for. This is a very simple but effective act that can immensely shift your perspective. Write down at least three things.

Let gratitude work its magic in your life, and watch as your stress transforms into strength. Another step closer to a stress-free life, kudos to you!

## DAY 4: HARMONIZING YOUR ENVIRONMENT

The state of your environment can largely impact your stress levels. Today's all about turning your personal spaces into a haven of tranquility.

## Recognizing Environmental Factors That Lead to Stress and Organizing Your Space

Identify elements in your surroundings that may evoke anxiety or mental unrest. It could be the clutter on your desk that is keeping you from thinking clearly. Or, maybe it's those pizza boxes in the corner of the kitchen that you meant to throw out yesterday. Whatever it is, be certain that your space is organized and conducive to a peaceful thought process.

## Implementing Sensory Relaxation Techniques

Anything from a soft blanket for touch, a vanilla-cinnamon scented candle for smell, or even some soft background music for hearing are great initiatives for sensory relaxation. You can add these fine touches to make your personal spaces sanctuaries of peace.

Always bear in mind calm and tranquil surroundings that translate to a serene state of mind. Till we meet again tomorrow!

## Day 5: Mindfulness in Motion

Day 5 revolves around embracing the beauty that mindfulness is and making every moment count.

## Integrating Mindfulness into Daily Activities and Fostering Present-Moment Awareness

Make a home for mindfulness in everything you do throughout the day. Be fully present in every moment. Be it brushing your teeth or sipping your morning latte. If you are eating, enjoy every single bite, taste the goodness, and feel the texture as you chew and eventually swallow the food. When walking, be mindful of every step as you connect with the ground beneath you. Be there to hear the sounds of the cars as they pass by, the birds as they chirp, or the raindrops as they collide with the zinc roofs. The aim is to just be one with the moment.

Remember that the true essence of life exists in the 'now', so cut off the dead weight of yesterday's regrets and tomorrow's fears. We meet again tomorrow!

## DAY 6: SET YOUR BOUNDARIES

Today's challenge is based on placing those much-needed boundaries to protect yourself against stress.

**Revisiting Boundaries**

Reflect on all your boundaries. Are they really serving their purpose? Are they really serving you? If not, reframe them.

**Assertiveness and Communication**

Being assertive is a vital part of your recovery. Today is the day when you gain the strength to start being assertive. Start by writing all the boundaries you want to assert and whom they are directed to.

**Saying 'No' as a Form of Self-Care**

Remember that you are a priority in your own life. It is important to say 'no' to commitments that overlap with your leisure time. Take today as your first step in mastering the art of saying no.

Love starts with you. If you cannot give yourself genuine love, then neither can you truly love someone else.

## DAY 7: CULTIVATE CONNECTIONS

Today's challenge is all about acknowledging the potency of genuine human bonds. Let us delve in.

### The Power of Social Bonds

Like medicine, social bonds have the capacity to strengthen our emotional armor. They promote a sense of togetherness and comfort you when times are dark.

### Rekindling Relationships

Today, try to reconnect with family or old friends whom you haven't communicated with in a long time. This can be a call or just a simple message.

### Lean On Your Support System

Is there something that is bothering you? Find a trusted family member or friend who you can talk it out with. Now is the time to start leaning on your social system.

**Reflection:** How did you feel after talking to others and putting yourself out there? How has it changed your perception of stressful matters?

Remember, as long as you aren't the only human left on Earth, you'll never have to stand on your own.

## DAY 8: MASTER YOUR TIME

Today's challenge focuses on taking ownership of your time. Organizing your day ahead of time not only catapults efficiency but also ensures that you have ample time for personal development.

**Revisit Chapter 8**

Start off by refreshing your memory on time management techniques and how they aid in stress relief.

**Crafting a Balanced Life**

Today, we aim to establish a seamless balance of work and leisure. With the techniques you learned on time management, put together a schedule that promotes both productivity and relaxation.

**Prioritize You**

Remember to leave open time blocks for you. Fit in hobbies and self-care activities into your calendar. What nourishes and re-energizes your soul is a priority.

## DAY 9: DEEPEN YOUR MINDFULNESS JOURNEY

Today's challenge centers on enhancing your mindfulness. With all the knowledge you've learned in this book, you will find a mindful activity that hits the sweet spot.

**Expand on Day 2**

Think back to the mindfulness activities you practiced earlier. How can you deepen your practice and connect better with the present moment?

**Exploring Meditation Styles**

Delve into the various avenues of mindfulness and find what works for you. It might be body scanning, mindful breathing, or sensory awareness. You have to discover what feels best.

**Identify Your Fit**

After experimenting, you should be able to pinpoint the meditation style that resonates with you and your needs.

## DAY 10: MOVE TO MANAGE STRESS

In today's challenge, you will be embracing the beauty of movement for the mind, body, and soul. It's all about immersing yourself in the joy of every stretch, step and sway.

**Exercise and Stress**

Revisit the sections of the book that discuss the stress-busting properties of stress.

**Explore New Activities**

Allow yourself to expand outside your comfort zone. Be it yoga, jogging, or Pilates, find something that will relinquish stress from your body.

**Everyday Movement**

Interweave movement into your daily schedule. This may be as simple as taking short breaks to walk, stretch, or even dance as you prepare a meal. Every day can look different.

## DAY 11: EMBRACE RESTFUL NIGHTS

Rest plays a critical role in stress recovery. This is why you need to make enough time to rest and recover after a long, tiring day of working.

**Understanding the Importance of Sleep**

Reflect on what you learned in the sections of the book that discuss sleep. Particularly on how getting quality sleep can help you manage your stress better.

**Establish a Calming Bedtime Routine**

Design a bedtime routine that is sure to get you to unwind. Try reading, gentle stretching, or playing calming background music to reinforce your sleepiness.

**Practice Relaxation Techniques**

Incorporate relaxation techniques such as mindfulness meditation before retiring to bed. Doing this will relax your mind and prepare you for a night of quality sleep. Don't look at any type of screen 30 minutes before bed (ex. phone, TV, or laptop).

Sleeping well is a crucial stress management tool that can take you very far in your journey. Good night and sweet dreams!

## DAY 12: FOSTER A GROWTH MINDSET

Today is all about fostering a mind that sees the glass that is half full and not half empty. As you start to grow, personally, a realization will set in that the tough obstacles that most of us dread is nothing but stepping stones to a better life.

## Discover Growth Mindset

Take time to reflect on how a growth mindset can change your perception of challenging situations. How can you develop a growth mindset that revolutionizes difficulties into opportunities?

## Challenge Limiting Beliefs

Think of all the limiting beliefs you may have, confront them, and replace them with more empowering beliefs.

## Celebrate Failures

Think of all your past failures as opportunities, not as setbacks. They are not dead ends but meaningful life lessons.

## DAY 13 CHALLENGE: EMBRACE CHANGE WITH A POSITIVE MINDSET

Today, we will reacquaint ourselves with the themes discussed in Chapter 10 and use them to propel us toward the stress-free life we've always yearned for.

## Revisiting Themes

Reflect on all the lessons and key insights encompassed by Chapter 10. What strategies and lessons did you resonate with the most? (The chapter talks about change, setting goals, and letting go.)

## Reflect on Personal Growth

Journal about how your life has transformed during this challenge. Are there any new habits that you have formed? Have you learned anything new about yourself? Once done, take a moment to yourself to celebrate your progress.

## Embrace Change Positively

Did you encounter any challenges during this challenge? If so, open up your arms and accept them wholeheartedly. Embrace the fact that everything that happened was for you and not against you.

Positivity is not extrinsic but intrinsic. Keep cultivating positive energy within you and watch as it transforms your entire life. Keep on going; you are almost there!

## DAY 14 CHALLENGE: SUSTAINING A STRESS-FREE LIFE

Today is a big day! Congratulations on making it to day 14 of the challenge. The goal of this day is to truly acknowledge your achievements, create a sustainable plan for stress management, and last but not least, foster a long-lasting sense of resilience.

### Acknowledging Achievements

Carve out time to reflect on everything you have accomplished throughout this challenge. What changes have you made, and how have they positively impacted your life? Celebrate all your successes and remember that smaller successes matter too.

### Creating a Sustainable Plan

Using the resources from this book, craft a plan to continue the stress relief practices that worked best for you. Incorporate them into your daily routine, ensuring they become lasting habits.

### Long-Term Resilience-Building

Venture into the future for a brief moment. How will you use the strategies you've learned in this book to build resilience against life's stressors? If needed, you can even consider seeking professional therapy.

You've learned valuable tools to lead a more stress-free life. Keep applying them, stay resilient, and remember that a stress-free life is an ongoing journey. Feel free to come back to the 14 day challenge often to help keep you on track. Well done!

Everything you learned in this chapter aims to prepare you for a more fulfilling, stress-free life. This information is your greatest ally and something you can always fall back on.

We have finally reached the end of this book, and I hope you have learned something profound from all of this. Let us now move into the conclusion, where we will recap on everything we discussed throughout the book.

# CONCLUSION

Before going any further, you should be extremely proud of yourself for fighting to the end. That, on its own, is a highly commendable job.

With all the knowledge you have gained in this book, you can start living the life of your dreams. All you need to do is believe that you can and trust the process. No more living in the dark, struggling to tell what is going on with your body and mind.

Since you now know clearly how stress manifests physically and mentally, stopping it from taking over your life has never been easier. Being able to spot signs of stress is one of the greatest skills you can have. This is because it not only protects you from the harm of stress itself but also the potential development of serious mental and physical illnesses.

Throughout the book, you learned several ways to reduce your stress. You must understand the fine art of mindfulness and how it can soothe your body in times of stress. It's truly amazing how a combination of conscious breaths and thoughts centered on the present moment can have such a positive impact on our health.

You learned about time management and the importance of making every minute count. With these skills at hand, you can now plan your time efficiently, get everything you need to get done, and still enjoy some quality time doing whatever brings joy to your soul.

You can say 'no more' to the days of being cooped up in isolation. From now on, you will be able to view your life through the lens of happiness and possibility. The doors are now open for you to go out there to experience the world without a sense of guilt or reservations.

All this is ahead of you if you believe it is. The most vital thing to be determined is in implementing and sustaining all the tips you have learned. Whether it is with meditation, therapy, or even physical exercise, showing up for yourself is always good, no matter how hard it may be.

Luckily, you have the 14-day challenge to help you reach your goals faster. This isn't something that should die down after two weeks, but rather a guideline on how you can develop habits that support a stress-free life.

There might be a friend, a colleague, or an uncle of yours who suffers from stress; be sure to let them in on this knowledge. Cheer them up with tips and strategies on how they can free themselves from stress and watch as their lives transform, too.

As we part ways, I wish you the best of luck in your journey going forth. Let it be immensely rewarding and fulfilling!

If you liked this book, please leave a review on Amazon.com!

# REFERENCES

Bakhuys Roozeboom, M. C., Schelvis, R. M. C., Houtman, I. L. D., Wiezer, N. M., & Bongers, P. M. (2020). Decreasing employees' work stress by a participatory, organizational level work stress prevention approach: A multiple-case study in primary education. *BMC Public Health, 20(1)*, 1–16. https://doi.org/10.1186/s12889-020-08698-2

Blain, T. (2022, June 23). *What are the physiological symptoms of stress?* Verywell Mind. https://www.verywellmind.com/physical-physiological-symptoms-of-stress-5270346

Cherney, K. (2020, November 3). *Therapy for Stress: What Works, Who to Work With, and Destressing ASAP.* Healthline. https://www.healthline.com/health/therapy-for-stress#therapies-for-stress

Cherry, K. (2023, March 3). *How social support contributes to psychological health.* Verywell Mind. https://www.verywellmind.com/social-support-for-psychological-health-4119970

Collado-Soler, R., Trigueros, R., Aguilar-Parra, J. M., & Navarro, N. (2023). Emotional intelligence and resilience outcomes in adolescent period, is knowledge really strength? Psychology Research and Behavior Management, *Volume 16*, 1365–1378. https://doi.org/10.2147/prbm.s383296

Doran, M. (2021, April 21). *Top foods to relieve stress.* Allina Health. https://www.allinahealth.org/healthysetgo/nourish/top-foods-to-relieve-stress

*8 exercises that relieve stress - women's guide to stress management.* (2011, May 11). Everyday Health. https://www.everydayhealth.com/exercise-photos/exercises-that-relieve-stress.aspx

*Exercising to relax.* (2020b, July 7). Harvard Health. https://www.health.harvard.edu/staying-healthy/exercising-to-relax

Marais, S. D. (2022, September 23). *5 cognitive symptoms of stress.* Psych

Central. https://psychcentral.com/stress/the-impact-of-stress#cognitive-skills-affected

Personnel Today. (2016, October 16). *Workplace stress: an occupational health case study*. RELX SDG Resource Centre. https://sdgresources.relx.com/articles-features/workplace-stress-occupational-health-case-study

Reid, S. (2023, March 2). *Social support for stress relief*. Help Guide. https://www.helpguide.org/articles/stress/social-support-for-stress-relief.

htm#:~:text=Research%20shows%20that%20people%20with

Reilly, S. E., Soulliard, Z. A., McCuddy, W. T., & Mahoney, J. J. (2021). *Frequency and perceived effectiveness of mental health providers' coping strategies during COVID-19*. Current Psychology. https://doi.org/10.1007/s12144-021-01683-x

Richardson, B. (2022, October 26). *Time Management Statistics & Facts (New 2022 Research)*. Acuity Training. https://www.acuitytraining.co.uk/news-tips/time-management-statistics-2022-research/#:~:text=Key%20Takeaways%20%E2%80%93%20-Time%20Management%20Statistics

*Stress in America 2020*. (2020, October). American Psychological Association. https://www.apa.org/news/press/releases/stress/2020/report-october

*Sleep hygiene tips- sleep and sleep disorders*. (2022, September 13). Centers for Disease Control and Prevention. https://www.cdc.gov/sleep/about_sleep/sleep_hygiene.html

*Understanding the stress response*. (2020, July 6). Harvard Health. https://www.health.harvard.edu/staying-healthy/understanding-the-stress-response

Wein, H. (2021, June 1). *Mindfulness for Your Health*. NIH News in Health. https://newsinhealth.nih.gov/2021/06/mindfulness-your-health#:~:text=Studies%20suggest%20that%20focusing%20on

Wiegner, L., Hange, D., Björkelund, C., & Ahlborg, G. (2015). Prevalence of perceived stress and associations to symptoms of exhaustion, depression and anxiety in a working age population seeking primary care. *BMC Family Practice,* *16*(1). https://doi.org/10.1186/s12875-015-0252-7